George Vance Smith

The spirit and the Word of Christ, and their permanent lessons

Second Edition

George Vance Smith

The spirit and the Word of Christ, and their permanent lessons
Second Edition

ISBN/EAN: 9783337260828

Printed in Europe, USA, Canada, Australia, Japan

Cover: Foto ©Lupo / pixelio.de

More available books at **www.hansebooks.com**

THE SPIRIT

AND

THE WORD OF CHRIST,

AND

THEIR PERMANENT LESSONS.

BY

G. VANCE SMITH, D.D., Ph.D.,

MINISTER OF ST. SAVIOURGATE CHAPEL, YORK.

"Now if any man have not the Spirit of Christ, he is none of his."
St. Paul, Rom. viii. 9.

"He that abideth in the doctrine of Christ, he hath both the Father and the Son."
St. John, Ep. 2, v. 9.

𝔖𝔢𝔠𝔬𝔫𝔡 𝔈𝔡𝔦𝔱𝔦𝔬𝔫, 𝔎𝔢𝔟𝔦𝔰𝔢𝔡 𝔞𝔫𝔡 𝔄𝔲𝔤𝔪𝔢𝔫𝔱𝔢𝔡.

LONDON:

LONGMANS, GREEN, AND CO.

1875.

PREFACE.

A LITTLE more than a year ago, it was proposed to me by a friend that I should write, and publish at his expense, a short account of the ministry of Christ, more especially as viewed in its practical, moral and religious aspects, and including some notice of such connected circumstances as might seem to illustrate the spirit and purpose of his teaching.

This task I undertook, but with a little hesitation, because I was not sure that my own idea of what was desired was exactly the same as that of its proposer; while circumstances which I need not state rendered it impracticable for us to communicate, except by letter. Such was the origin of the present little work, which, as I wrote, I soon found it impossible to compress within the limits of a Tract of twenty or thirty pages, as had been at first contemplated. I received, however, perfect liberty in regard to the size to which the work might run; while yet it was desirable to remember distinctly the leading motive for its preparation, —to obtain a short exposition, simply written, and suitable for the use of unlearned readers more particularly. This purpose I have kept in view throughout, even though led so far beyond the limits originally thought of; and the work is now published not as a Tract, but as a substantive volume.

Alas, I must add, the friend who interested himself about it, as I have mentioned, has not been spared to see its completion. He died, not many weeks ago, leaving a name and an example of Christian well-doing widely and affectionately remembered in the community amidst which he had lived, and such as will not fail to recommend the object which he had at heart to all who knew him, far more persuasively than any poor words of mine.

I need scarcely say that, in what I have written, it has been my earnest desire to exhibit the Teaching and Spirit of Christ simply as they *were*, without exaggeration, negative or positive. I have sought to observe the just mean between over-criticism on the one hand, and the strange and superstitious extremes of popular orthodoxy on the other. I may add, that the effect of my inquiries and reflections in writing this book has wholly been to strengthen my own feelings of reverence towards the Christian Master. It has also been to give me a more unbounded confidence that, in returning to the simplicity of his words, and making these more entirely than heretofore the foundation on which to build not only our churches but even other organizations of civilized life, will be found the true solution for some of the most urgent and perplexing problems of our time.*

February, 1874.

For the present edition the work has been carefully revised, many slight alterations having been introduced, chiefly for the sake of increased clearness of expression. In one case an addition of greater length has been made—viz., in the Appendix, Note F., on the interpretation of John viii. 58.

Good Friday, 1875.

* On many of the topics which are only slightly touched in the following pages, or which, within so short a space, it was not possible to touch at all, I would beg to refer the reader to another little work of my own "The Bible and Popular Theology: a Re-statement of Truths and Principles, with special Reference to recent Works of Dr. Liddon, Lord Hatherley, the Right Hon. W. E. Gladstone, and Others" (Third Edition, 1871).

"   . . . wheresoe'er
Christ's spirit breathes a holier air;
Where Christlike faith is keen to seek
What Truth or Conscience freely speak;
Where Christlike love delights to span
The rents that sever man from man;
Where round God's throne His just ones stand,
There, Christian, is thy native land!"

DEAN STANLEY.

CONTENTS.

CHAPTER I.

Introductory—Sources of the Evangelical history—Their chronological order—Substance of their statements—The miraculous conception—Materials used by the first three Evangelists—Similarity of plan — Citation of Scripture — The fourth Gospel 1

CHAPTER II.

The earlier period of the Ministry—Political circumstances—The Early training of Jesus Christ – Popular influences—John the Baptist — Messianic expectations — The Temptation—The Miracles—Essential principle of allegiance to Christ . . 14

CHAPTER III.

The teaching of Christ—Illustrative considerations—The Pharisees—Writings of the Prophets—The Sermon on the Mount —Letter and Spirit—Precepts of limited application—Non-resistance—Riches and poverty 28

CHAPTER IV.

The teaching of Christ (continued)—Religious principles—The Christian idea of God—Love to God and man—Absence of dogma—Condemnation of formalism — Human nature—Future retribution—Explanation of words—Eternal Fire—Prayer—Christian Anthropomorphism 41

CHAPTER V.

The final scenes—The entry into Jerusalem—The Messiahship of Jesus, its true character—The Lord's Supper—Gethsemane—The Trial and Crucifixion—Singular omission in the Evangelical narrative—The great Example, was it real? . . 57

CHAPTER VI.

The Atonement or Reconciliation by the Death of Christ—Ancient ideas—The Gentile controversy and its determination—Man reconciled to God, not God to man—Sense in which Christ died for sin—Absence of orthodox ideas—Figurative expressions—"For Christ's sake"—The Epistle to the Hebrews . 70

CHAPTER VII.

The Word made flesh—Differences between the first three Gospels and the fourth—True character of this Gospel—The Word or Logos—Origin of the conception—Dr. Liddon's account of it—Peculiar expressions—The "Only" God—The Nicene Creed 87

CHAPTER VIII.

Baptism—The threefold formula—Its original meaning—Not used in the New Testament—Changes in modern times—The Anglican doctrine—Unknown to the apostles—Baptismal Regeneration—Not believed by many, though professed—Godfathers and godmothers—Immersion or sprinkling—True import of the Service 100

CHAPTER IX.

Permanent element in the life of Christ—Some early beliefs have passed away—Mr. Gladstone on the Essential Truths of Christianity—His statement criticised—The Spirit of Christ, the imperishable essence of his religion—True basis for the Christian Church—Church authority—Hope for the future . 114

CHAPTER X.

Fallacies and objections—From the positive or orthodox side—From the negative side—The objection to miracles—Necessity of discrimination—The loyalty due to Christ—Our duty still 127

APPENDIX.

A.—Non-Christian testimonies respecting Jesus Christ . . 137
B.—Pauline passages which appear to speak of Jesus Christ as God:—Rom. ix. 5, Philip. ii. 6 140
C.—On Acts xx. 28, John i. 18, 1 John v. 20 . . . 145
D.—On Titus ii. 13, 2 Peter i. 1 147
E.—The titles "Son of Man" and "Son of God" . . 148
F.—On the interpretation of John viii. 58 . . . 153

THE SPIRIT AND THE WORD OF CHRIST.

CHAPTER I.

INTRODUCTORY—SOURCES OF THE EVANGELICAL HISTORY.

THE earliest materials for the life of Christ belong exclusively to the pages of the New Testament.* As found there, they may be classed under three heads,—the Epistles, the first three or synoptical Gospels, the writings attributed to St. John. This order corresponds, in a general way, to the periods from which the respective documents are believed to come down—excepting the book of Revelation, which is most probably one of the earlier books; excepting also

* The brief allusions to the Founder of Christianity contained in Suetonius, Tacitus, and Pliny, form no exception to this statement. Nor does the very notable passage in Josephus, which, moreover, is too much exposed to the suspicion of having been interpolated to be used as historical evidence. But see Appendix, Note A.

some of the smaller epistles, which are of late date and uncertain authorship.

The principal Epistles, those of St. Paul, were written between the years 52 and 62, A.D. The first three Gospels belong to a time not less than twenty years later; the writings of John to a yet later date, probably near the close of the first century. Some investigators, it is well known, assign the fourth Gospel to the second century; but the point is one which cannot be suitably discussed in this place. Whatever may be ultimately established as to the authorship and date of this document, there can be no doubt that its origin belongs to an early period of Christian antiquity, though not to the earliest. Nor can there be a question, that it represents a conception of the person and work of Christ which was widely held even in the second century, and which has proved, in the result, to be one of the great forces in determining the character of dogmatic Christianity as now received.

The information afforded by the New Testament respecting the personal ministry of Christ is what chiefly concerns our present object. Taking the sources of that information in the order above indicated, we may derive from the larger epistles some of the leading facts of our Lord's career, though, it will be seen, by no means so clear or so ample an account as may be found in the Gospels. The words of St. Paul are the most to our purpose. That apostle was well acquainted with Jerusalem, and with its leading men. He had no personal intercourse with the TEACHER,* but it is plain, both from his own writings and from the Acts, that he stood in very close connection with those who had known him, and with some also of the apostles.† Paul was brought up as a Pharisee, and was, in the first instance, an enemy and a persecutor of the new sect of the Nazarenes. He must therefore have been well informed of all that could be said against Jesus and his followers. Yet he became a disciple; and, so far as can be judged, he was the most zealous and successful of all the early preachers of the Gospel. There is reason to believe that he sacrificed his life in the work to which he thus devoted himself.

This apostle, it is evident, could have given no stronger testimony than he did give of his Christian faith, or of his love and reverence towards the Christian Master. Indeed, almost every chapter of his writings is a witness to this effect; and we may well believe that the personal qualities and attested words

---

* Jesus is repeatedly thus styled in all the Gospels:—*e.g.* Matt. xii. 38; Mark x. 17; Luke x. 25; John xiii. 13. That he should *teach* the people, was evidently a part of the popular conception of the Messiah's office. The fact is unfortunately everywhere disguised in the authorized version by the rendering *Master*.

† Acts xxi. 16–18.

and deeds which, by their transmitted influence, could inspire and satisfy such a mind as Paul's, and lead him to give himself up as he did to the work of an apostle, must have been of the highest moral character. The testimony of St. Paul to Christ is evidently, therefore, of very great importance.

The following are the leading points to which the apostle alludes, and which, it will be seen, are in substantial harmony with the fuller details of the Evangelists. He refers to the fact that Jesus was descended from the line of David, and states or implies that he was received by many as the expected Messiah; that he lived in circumstances of poverty and humiliation; that he selected apostles, who were engaged in preaching the Gospel after his death; that on the last evening of his life, he partook of the Passover with the Twelve, and instituted the Lord's Supper; that his life and the spirit of his life were of such conspicuous purity and uprightness as made him worthy to be an example to his followers and to all the world; that he was put to death, buried, raised again, and seen after his resurrection by many of the disciples, as at a later period by the apostle himself. Such are the circumstances which clearly appear in the Epistles of Paul, as may be learnt by the references given below.*

* Rom. i. 3, 4; 2 Cor. viii. 9; Phil. ii. 6–8; 1 Cor. xii.; Gal. iii. 13; 1 Cor. xi. 23, *seq.*; 2 Cor. v. 21; 1 Cor. xv. 1–4; 1 Thess. ii. 15; Rom. xiii. 14; Ephes. iv. 13–15; Coloss. iii. 1, *seq.*

The substance of Paul's Christianity, in other words of the 'Gospel' which he preached, was unquestionably the Messiahship of Jesus. This, to the apostle's mind, was closely connected with, or dependent upon, his resurrection, and involved also the belief in his return at a future period to assume his Messianic kingdom, to sit in judgment upon a sinful world, and receive his faithful followers to share in the privileges and glories of his own exaltation. The latter was the 'salvation' revealed through Christ, and to which even Gentiles might be admitted by 'faith,' that is, by their belief and acceptance of Jesus as the Messiah. Some of these particulars are simply part of the apostle's idea and interpretation of the Gospel, and are not to be reckoned among the outward facts with which we are now more immediately concerned. It will be the purpose of a later section of this work to trace the distinction between temporary or transient conceptions and what has been shown by results to be possessed of a more solid and durable character.

The particulars which may be thus learnt from Paul are confirmed by what is read in other epistles, as that of James, the First of Peter, and the epistle to the Hebrews. James has evidently the humility of Christ in his view, when he exhorts his readers to consideration for the poor man, and to other good works, on the strength of the equal admission of the poor to the kingdom of heaven. Peter, if he wrote the first of the Epistles called after him, and the author of the writing to the Hebrews, who is not certainly known to us, both refer to the sufferings of Christ, the former laying especial stress upon his patience, meekness, and submission, in the final scenes of his life.*

There are two or three instances in the English version of the New Testament in which St. Paul will appear to most readers to add to the foregoing a particular of the very highest importance. He appears to speak of Jesus Christ as *God*.† For a short discussion of these passages, as well as of some others which appear to convey the same idea, the reader is referred to the Appendix. To this also may conveniently be postponed an explanation of the two very frequent Messianic appellations of Jesus, the terms " Son of Man " and "Son of God."‡

The details which may thus be gleaned from the Epistles are of especial value, because they are found in the earliest period of the primitive Christian history to which it is possible to ascend by documentary evidence. They are also recorded by those who either knew the Lord in their own persons, or else had received what they tell us from others who did so. Of this there can be no reasonable doubt. The same

---

* James ii. 1-7; Heb. v. 7; 1 Pet. ii. 21-23.
† Rom. ix. 5; Philip. ii. 6; 1 Tim. iii. 16.
‡ Appendix, Notes B, C, D, E.

particulars manifestly agree with the more detailed accounts of the Gospels, and serve to give weight to these. And yet it must be admitted they are not sufficient to afford anything like a complete view of the Author of Christianity. Had we nothing more from the first century, our knowledge would be meagre in the extreme; and we could only wonder that so great a power had arisen in the world, and left behind it so few indications of its own actual origin and personal character.

. The synoptical Gospels, considerably later in point of time* than the Epistles above referred to, supply us in large measure with the details which are needed to fill up the outline suggested by the earlier documents. Two of the synoptists give us information respecting the parentage and birth of Jesus. The statements which they have preserved on these points do not, however, agree; showing that the accounts which they followed were most probably of late origin, and not founded upon the exact facts of the case on one side or the other, or perhaps on both. Let any one carefully compare the first two chapters of

* By this expression it is simply intended to refer to the existing form of the Gospels, but by no means to exclude the idea of their containing materials, that is, incorporated and written statements, which are still older than the oldest of the Epistles. One of the great problems of the criticism of the Gospels, is to distinguish between the older and the later portions of their contents.

Matthew, as they lie before us, with those of Luke, and he will scarcely fail to see the correctness of this statement. The whole subject is of subordinate importance, but two things are worthy of particular notice.

In the *first* place, the introductory chapters of Matthew and Luke have somewhat the appearance of being a separate document added on to each Gospel, and not originally a part of it. Certain statements of early Church writers, respecting these Gospels, favour this view of the subject. In the *second* place, it is remarkable that the miraculous birth, so conspicuously introduced at the beginning of Matthew and Luke, is never again referred to throughout the New Testament. Extraordinary as this section of the history is, no subsequent use is made of it. Paul not only does not allude to it, but, on the contrary, he speaks of Jesus as shown to be the Christ, not by his miraculous birth, but by his resurrection from the dead.[*] The fourth Evangelist is equally silent as to the same wonderful incident, although it would have been highly suitable, at the commencement of his narrative, to have at least alluded to it. However, such omissions, here and elsewhere, may be explained, they at least serve to show us that the miraculous birth was but little thought of by the disciples of Paul's time. May we not even think,

[*] Rom. i. 4.

that at the time when he wrote, it had not yet emerged into notice, and was altogether a later product of the evangelical tradition?

Of both the Gospels just referred to it may, however, be observed, that the accounts which they give of the birth of Jesus have a peculiar corroborative value, even though admitted to have been written at a late period, and to have grown up without any solid foundation of fact. They clearly attest the high and unusual character of the life of Christ, as this was looked back upon by the generation following his own, or the one which came after that. They suggest to us also the great moral and religious excellence of his teaching. For it is plain that nothing else could have warranted or given occasion to a narrative which attributed his birth to the supernatural interposition of the Divine Spirit itself. In this respect, again, the two accounts stand on very much the same ground as the conception of the Logos in the fourth Gospel. This, too, affords a testimony of the most striking kind to the moral and spiritual greatness of Jesus Christ.

The three synoptics agree with each other in a remarkable way, not only in the general outlines in which they present to us the ministry of Christ, but also in their numerous instances of verbal coincidence. Their harmony of outline is explained by the fact that the early tradition, written or oral, which they have incorporated, was in the main, though with many discrepancies, a *true* representation. For the verbal coincidences and diversities, when minutely examined, it is often more difficult to account.* Nor can the subject be properly discussed within our present limits. It seems probable that each synoptist in writing his Gospel made a free use of materials already existing, some of them, beyond question, in a written form. These, by the nature of the case, would necessarily be largely the *same* materials,—as accumulated within the interval since the death of Christ,—a period of from forty to fifty years, or more. Within this long interval there was space enough for the origin of much diversity of narrative, both oral and written, or even for the growth of statements diverging, in important degrees, from the primitive fact. It is most desirable, for the sake of Christianity itself, and even from a due regard to the moral and intellectual character of Jesus, that this should not be lost sight of. It is unwise to neglect it, in the way exemplified by some recent historians,†—quite as much so as it would be to rely upon the old theory of verbal inspiration. The latter, in the face of well-known *facts*, is wholly

---

* Coincidences in the words of Christ were evidently to be expected, and those portions of the three synoptics in which they occur should probably be regarded as the most ancient parts of each.

† The reader may compare Pressensé's *Jesus Christ* (4th ed., 1871), book i., iv. 3; book ii., i. 1.

untenable, and tends only to discredit Christianity itself, in the judgment of many,—friends and foes alike.

If the three synoptics are compared with one another, they will be seen to be constructed on a very definite plan, which, in general terms, is the same in each. From the birth of Jesus each writer goes on, more or less fully, to relate (1) the baptism and its connected circumstances; (2) the temptation, which in Mark is given with extreme brevity; (3) the ministry of Christ in Galilee; (4) the journey from Galilee to Jerusalem, to the Passover; (5) the entry into Jerusalem in the publicly assumed character of Messiah; (6) the final events, ending with the crucifixion and resurrection.

It will be seen that, with this general resemblance in regard to plan, there is great diversity among the three writers in the details which they have given. In the midst of much verbal agreement (especially, as might be expected, in the words of Jesus), there is great variety and difference—whole discourses and parables being reported by one, not by another. Thus it is, for example, with the collection of beautiful parables and connected incidents found in Luke, from ix. 51 to xix. 28, and which are only found in this Gospel. It would appear, therefore, that each writer, while often using materials common to the others, was yet in possession of matter peculiar to himself, or has, at least, for his own reasons, chosen to incorporate matter which the others have as freely decided to put aside, if they had it. Moreover, it is clear they cannot have intended to give a careful chronological *history* of events, in the sense in which we should now understand this term—a sense of the word, probably, of which they had hardly thought. Each Evangelist had no doubt a special object in view in writing. This was, to record and illustrate what he believed to be the *truth*, namely, that Jesus of Nazareth was the expected Christ. This he sought, therefore, to set forth, not only by the selection of such incidents from the personal life of Jesus as appeared to be best suited for his purpose, but also by the citation of such Old Testament passages as seemed to be applicable to the same end.

The idea under which the latter was done may have been something like the following. Jesus, to the conviction of his biographers, had been shown to be the Messiah. It was, therefore, a matter of course that every Old Testament passage usually understood to refer to that expected personage would be applicable to him, and to the incidents of his career. Hence the constant citation of the words of the Hebrew Scriptures (mostly from the Septuagint translation of them); and hence, too, it must be added, their frequent application, in meanings which cannot have been *intended* by the original writers.* Such, however, was the custom of the time; and it always remains to be determined by a due consideration of each case, whether or not a New Testament writer or speaker cites a passage of the ancient books in its original sense, or only in a kind of secondary sense, suggested by the circumstances in reference to which it is brought forward. Some considerable difficulties in the interpretation of the Christian books may be obviated, if this reasonable principle be kept in view.

Of the Gospel of John, as one of the primary sources of the history of Jesus, it will be most convenient and satisfactory to speak in a subsequent chapter. For the present it may be sufficient to observe that John's account cannot, in my own judgment, be truly harmonized with the synoptics, as regards either the subject matter or the literary form into which the narrative has been cast. Nevertheless, it is evident the fourth Evangelist wrote for the very same object which the three synoptists had before them,—to show that Jesus of Nazareth was the expected Christ.† He did so, however, in his own peculiar manner, and according to his own conception of the relation between Christ and God,

---

* As, *e.g.*, when St. Paul cites the words of Ps. xix. 4, to show that the Gospel was to be preached to all the world: Rom. x. 18. Compare also Acts i. 20 with Ps. lxix. 25, cix. 8.

† John xx. 31.

and these were, in some important respects, different from theirs. This question, however, we shall be enabled to take up with greater advantage in a later part of this work.

In regard to the book of Acts, it is enough in the present connection to observe that it is in substantial agreement with the history of Jesus, as found in the synoptics. This may be seen, for example, in the speech of Peter in chapter ii.; but, with one apparent exception,* the book makes no addition to the synoptical narratives which require special notice.

CHAPTER II.

THE EARLIER PERIOD OF THE MINISTRY OF CHRIST.

THE interval from the birth of Christ to the commencement of his public career lies between the years B.C. 4 and A.D. 27,—the nativity having taken place somewhat before the date commonly assigned. It was one of the most notable epochs which the world has seen. The Roman empire had nearly attained its widest limits, no existing power having been able to offer a successful resistance to its

---

* Acts xx. 28. See Appendix, Note C.

disciplined forces. Several features in the civilization of the day tended to favour the growth and diffusion of a new religion. The old superstitions were worn out, and mostly abandoned, by thoughtful persons, to the ignorant multitudes. The progress of the Roman arms and of commerce had opened out the means of communication with distant regions, while the Greek and Latin languages formed an excellent medium of literary and commercial intercourse, for peoples otherwise effectually separated from each other. At the same time, the dispersion of the Jews and the existence of synagogues in some of the principal centres of Roman power, obviously tended to the same result. The 'fulness of time' was thus come, when it would be possible for the promulgators of a new religion to make their way throughout the world more easily and rapidly than at any earlier period,—an advantage of which the Christian preachers were not slow to avail themselves.

The interval of about thirty years now more particularly referred to is, however, but slightly touched by the evangelical narrative. One incident only is recorded in connection with Jesus. It is his visit to Jerusalem at the age of twelve years, and his being found by his parents listening to the doctors and asking them questions. There is nothing improbable in the occurrence, unless it be the length of time during which the boy was separated from his friends. We must remember how brief and fragmentary is the narrative, which must have been written many years after the event. It is most probable that the narrator intended us to understand that he of whom he was speaking was beginning, even at so early an age, to be sensible of the peculiar work to which he was called. *He* was conscious of this, though his parents were not; while yet his mother, like a true mother, cherished in her heart the words of her first-born son.*

In the long period during which Jesus is now lost to sight, we are left to infer that he lived with his parents in the obscure and ill-reputed little town of Nazareth. This place, unimportant as it was, was not without its advantages for the training of the future Christ. In that northern border-land, he would be brought into contact with people of Gentile birth, and with Samaritans; and he would doubtless, in this personal intercourse, learn to cherish towards them the just and kindly feeling which afterwards appeared in his teachings. He is often spoken of in the Gospels as a Nazarene; in one case as 'the prophet Jesus from Nazareth.'† It is easy to see that his circumstances were comparatively humble, like those of his nearest relatives; and very probably he worked with his father at the trade of a

* Luke ii. 7. † Matt. xxi. 11.

carpenter.* There is an ancient tradition in one of the early Fathers to the same effect.

Yet it is also easy to understand that the youth, as he grew up, would receive the usual instruction given to their sons by devout parents of Jewish race. His mind would be stored, as we knew it was, with the lessons of their ancient law and religion. He would become familiar with the great examples and events of their past history. He would join in the services of the synagogue, and be taught to reverence the words of prophets and holy men of old which he would there hear, as they were read aloud, time after time, through many years. Thus, too, growing up, as he did, amidst 'the common people' of his day, he would share in their patriotic feelings, in their hopes for the coming of the kingdom of God, the diffusion of the true religion in the earth, and the destruction or expulsion from the sacred soil of Palestine of their heathen oppressors. There is no evidence whatever to show us that Jesus, in his earlier years, did not partake in this way of the peculiar feelings, ideas, knowledge, and ignorance of his people; or, rather, there is every reason, from his recorded history, to believe that he did so.†

The remembrance of this will relieve us from sundry difficulties in the reported words of Christ. As

* Matt. xiii. 55; Mark vi. 3.
† Comp. Mark xiii. 32; Luke ii. 52.

examples to this effect, may be mentioned the belief that certain diseases were caused by evil spirits, or demons, in the afflicted person; and also the manner in which the ancient Scriptures are often cited by Christ himself, and said to be fulfilled in events or persons of the time. The former belief was widely prevalent among the ancients, not only in Palestine, but in other parts of the world; and we know how the Jews esteemed their Scriptures beyond all other books, employing them, as before pointed out, precisely in the way which Christ himself frequently exemplifies.

It is interesting and instructive in the highest degree to recall how entirely our Lord was thus one of the people,—one, I may even say, of the ordinary working men of his time;* and how the divine Providence of the world chose, in this case, to act wonderfully among the nations, not by the medium of the great or learned of the earth—a philosopher, a poet, or a politician of Athens, or Rome, or Alexandria—but by the very humblest instrumentality which could perhaps have been employed—even by one of lowly birth, residing in a rude and despised district of a remote province of the Roman empire. This consideration, it is clear, ought to give to Christianity—

---

* We may notice the very striking illustration of this given in Mr. Holman Hunt's well-known picture, 'The Shadow of Death.'

that is to say, to the teaching of its Founder—all the stronger hold upon the masses of the people of these days. The working men of our own country, in turning away, as so many of them do, with distrust or dislike from Christ, as if he were but the representative of the priestly or aristocratic spirit, are turning away in fact from one of their own class, from one who thoroughly sympathized with the poor, the suffering, and the oppressed; and whose precepts and spirit, if followed as they deserve to be, would go far to render the life even of the humblest sons of toil a thing of comeliness and honour in the sight of God and man. And not only was Jesus himself one of this class of persons; his apostles were mostly the same: as if the great Disposer would show us that, in them, He designed to raise and dignify human labour, and lead us even to observe that it is an especial object of his blessing.

The period of obscurity and preparation at length passed; and the young man of Nazareth emerged into the full light of day, and speedily began to attract the notice of those around him.

The occasion on which he is first presented to us was an unusual one. It was during the time when the Baptist stood forth to proclaim the near approach of the kingdom of God. The burden of his preaching was Repentance. 'Repent,' he said, ' for the kingdom of heaven is at hand '—and multitudes, we are told, went out to hear what so strange a messenger had to announce. From this section of the evangelical history we may learn something of the moral condition of the Jewish people at the time. It appears that the preacher was little satisfied with what he knew of those who came to him. Pharisees and Sadducees, equally with meaner people, were received with an earnest rebuke for their wickedness, and a warning to flee from the wrath to come; while to the soldiers and those called publicans was given a similar lesson.

It is thus evident that, in the Baptist's case, as in that of the prophets of old, what was enjoined as a preparation for the kingdom of heaven was practical moral uprightness; that doing of the will of God which, we are often told, is more acceptable to Him than burnt-offerings and sacrifices. John was in this respect a worthy forerunner of the Master himself; a true voice from on high, crying in the wilderness, and making the way straight for that greater messenger whose shoe-lachet he deemed himself not worthy to unloose.

It is not difficult to understand how the preaching of John may have been a great determining influence in the life of Christ. As the Providential designs are often worked out by humble human instruments, so now it doubtless was; the mind of the hitherto obscure 'carpenter's son' was aroused, by the call of the prophet, into a deeper consciousness of the spiritual powers which slumbered within him. John was expecting the appearance of the Christ, very probably under the impulse of the popular belief of his day; which told him that this great personage would unite in himself the virtues and the dignity of a faithful servant of God, and be at the same time one to whom none could be acceptable subjects except those who shared and aspired after his own righteousness. Other ideas were also associated with the high character of this long looked-for Prince. He was to be possessed of divine powers which should enable him, at the head of victorious hosts, to vanquish and cast out of the land the ungodly strangers who now polluted the holy city with their presence. This conception of the Messianic office, no doubt, widely prevailed among the Jews; nor is it surprising, or rather it is perfectly in accordance with that human nature which all allow him to have possessed, that Jesus himself should have been under the influence of these popular ideas. This also it is reasonable to infer from the nature of the temptations to which it is recorded that he was exposed at the commencement of his ministry.

The form in which this part of the narrative* is written is largely due to the ideas of the time in regard to the origin of evil, and of temptation in par-

* Matt iv. 1-11; Luke iv. 1-13.

ticular. The belief in a great prince of darkness was an ancient belief of the Oriental nations. It is scarcely met with in the Old Testament, and nowhere in the oldest books,* nor was it, so far as is known, an influential element in the Hebrew religion of the times preceding the captivity. But it existed among the Assyrians, the Persians, and other peoples of their part of the world; and it was introduced among the Hebrews, or its influence was confirmed among them, by their intercourse with those foreign races.

In the time of Christ the belief in Satan and in bad spirits was firmly fixed among his people. It was natural, therefore, or inevitable, to any writer of that age, in speaking of evil thoughts and temptations, to attribute these to their suggestion.† Jesus, then, we may easily understand, did not enter upon the work to which he felt himself called, without some natural hesitation within his mind as to the true character of the course before him. Even the inducement

---

* A peculiar conception of Satan occurs in Job (i., ii.) Zech. (iii. 1, 2), 1 Chron. xxi. 1,—all, including this part of Zechariah, of comparatively late date.

† The words of the Lord's Prayer, 'Deliver us from evil,' were, by the Church Fathers taken to mean, 'Deliver us from the evil *one*.' There is no actual necessity for this rendering, nor is it, perhaps, even justifiable on exegetical grounds. But, unquestionably, the words, so understood, would be in harmony with the belief of our Lord himself and his contemporaries.

to apply to some temporal need of his own the powers which he felt to be within his command, would appear to have been no stranger to his mind. If, for example, he were at some time in want of food, whether in the wilderness or elsewhere, might he not think that he could employ his Messianic power to provide for the necessities of the moment? But such a use of the talent with which he had been entrusted was not, he would reflect, the true purpose for which it had been given. 'Man doth not live by bread alone,' but also by the command, the will, and the inspiration of the great Giver.

In the same devout spirit, he was sure that he must not use even for self-preservation what had been entrusted to him for other and greater ends. The temptation to do so might be fitly met by the thought that he must not commit any rash act even in dependence on Divine protection; and this too is expressed in the words of Scripture, 'Thou shalt not tempt the Lord thy God.' When, again, he felt the strength of those temporal hopes which filled the hearts of the people, it would easily occur to him to direct his efforts, and his growing influence with those around him, in such a way as to bring about their fulfilment. But this ambition to possess 'the kingdoms of the world and the glory of them,' was not to be realized without a virtual departure from the immediate service of God; and was it not written, 'Thou shalt worship the Lord thy God, and Him only shalt thou serve?'

It is impossible, in the light of modern knowledge, to accept, as it stands, the narrative of these incidents, regarded as a literal history of actual facts. Nevertheless, the writer of it most probably intended it to be so understood. Looking back, through the long interval of many years, upon the commencement of the ministry of which he was about to speak, and designing to notice the doubts and temptations by which it was known that Jesus had, at this period, been assailed, he would naturally put his statement into the form in which we have it. The temptations, then, may have been real; doubtless, they were so; and without question they were needed to bring out the latent strength and sensibility of the mind upon which they fell. Moreover, as in most cases of the kind, the tried and tempted soul, standing firm and triumphing at last over the insidious foe, would remain in the end with a more assured sense of moral power, a clearer and more animating confidence in Divine protection. Such 'angels' of heaven would not fail to 'come and minister' to it. But, manifestly, the *form* of the narrative in which all this is related is due to the temporary beliefs of the age; and by no means requires from us an assent to that dreadful tenet of the popular orthodoxy which tells us of the existence of an all but omnipotent Satan, who, in the contest between him and God, which is even now going on in the soul and life of every human being, is very commonly victorious.

We have now reached the period at which Jesus entered upon his more active work. He 'began to preach, and to say, Repent; for the kingdom of heaven is at hand.' It would seem that at first he simply followed in the Baptist's steps, uttering in substance the same call to repentance which had issued from his lips, and again suggesting to us, in no doubtful way, the regard for duty, the moral and religious fidelity, the righteousness in thought and in deed, by which the follower of Christ must be animated.

But his course was speedily attended by consequences of which there is no trace in connection with John. The fame of his preaching was spread abroad, and the people followed him in crowds, including those whom, in the first instance, he specially summoned to his side, who 'left their nets and followed him,' and eventually became his apostles.

The age-enduring character of the influence thus acquired by Jesus of Nazareth is one of the greatest marvels of history. The explanation of it afforded by the Gospels is familiar to all the world. He was 'a man attested of God, ... by mighty works and wonders and signs which God did by him.' Admitting this, and that the Unsearchable Spirit, for his own great ends, called the people of those days to new spiritual life in so unusual a way, we may understand why he who was thus distinguished among men was followed by the multitudes; why, notwithstanding outward appearances, he was regarded by many as the long expected Christ, and spoken of by his biographers, as by Paul and others before them, as possessed of that character. We can understand why even his death, followed, as it was, by the continued disappointment of long-cherished hopes of his second coming, could not put an end to his influence. We can understand how it might be that some features of an improbable or obviously mythical character became mixed up, in the course of time, with the evangelical narratives.* Things of this kind may be easily accounted for, while yet enough is left to explain the wonderful consequences which so speedily resulted from the ministry of Jesus.

But there are many who think they can account for the whole story, and all its train of wonders, without the admission of anything extraordinary, of the kind now alluded to. Such inquirers will follow their own explanation, and have a right to do so. It is certainly easy, from the nature of the case, to pull the written narrative to pieces; to point out how artlessly it is put together; what chronological and other

---

* As, for example, the accounts of the miraculous birth, and compare Matt. xxvii. 53, 54; Mark v. 11–16.

difficulties it involves; and how, in short, we ought not to rely upon it as a credible history of anything whatever. Those who see reason and are satisfied to do this, will do it. Any such persons may, nevertheless, I hope, be religious and Christ-like in spirit and in conduct; they may honour the name of Christian, and desire, therefore, to claim it for themselves. It may be that they are often even better entitled to bear it than many a so-called disciple, who, while believing, or professing to believe, everything, only discredits his profession by the mean or selfish or godless character of his life. It is not for one to judge another on this point, or to shut out from the number of disciples any that may desire to come in and be included. Let us, in a word, therefore gladly confess that the true substance of Christian allegiance consists far less in what a man may find himself able to believe, as the result of honest investigation about the details of the personal history of Christ, than in striving faithfully to receive and obey his precepts and imitate the spirit of his life.

And this conclusion, if it be a right one, ought to settle the question now raised in some quarters, whether or not a 'Theist' is or can be a Christian, and fairly entitled to bear that honoured name. Surely Christ himself was a 'Theist,' and the greatest of all that have ever been entitled to be so called. He, too, it is certain, would not have excluded from his fold any man or woman whatever who seeks and strives to love and worship God, and to keep his commandments. For did he not even say, 'Whosoever shall do the will of my Father which is in heaven, the same is my brother and sister and mother?'*

CHAPTER III.

FORM AND SUBSTANCE OF OUR LORD'S TEACHING: PRACTICAL PRECEPTS.

It is not necessary for the purposes of this work to recall with any minuteness the political or other circumstances of Judea in the time of Christ; but a few particulars of this kind will help us the better to read his words in the sense which his hearers and contemporaries would put upon them.

The reign of Herod the Great was long past when he began his ministry. But the violent and unscrupulous character of that king cannot have been without its evil influence in the countries over which he ruled. It is not surprising, therefore, to find in the New Testament, long afterwards, many indications of the low moral and physical condition of the Jewish people of those times. These are seen in the pictures of disease, poverty, lawlessness, presented or suggested at various points in the narrative, as, for example, in some of the parables and miracles, in the circum-

* Matt. xii. 50.

stances attending the death of the Baptist, in the stoning of Stephen, and in the crucifixion.

In the time of Christ, the dominions of Herod had been partitioned among his sons, of whom we have but slight glimpses in the New Testament. What we see of their character is not prepossessing. One of them, at the instigation of his paramour, put John the Baptist to death; and it is clear that the ruling men of the time in Palestine, whether Jewish or Roman, were men to whom bloodshed, sensuality, and tyranny were not unfamiliar.

In such circumstances, it was natural for all faithful Israelites to cling the more firmly to the ancient hope of the deliverer to come. The character of this expected personage has been already briefly pointed out. It is well also to bear in mind that he was to ' redeem his people from their sins,' an expression which included the evil fortune which their sins were conceived to have brought upon them. It was doubtless owing to the failure of Jesus to satisfy the latter expectation, that a section of the people were so ready at last to turn against him as they did, and cry aloud for his crucifixion.

Of the leading parties among the Jews, the Pharisees and the Sadducees are the most prominent. The former alone claim a few words of notice, as, at this time, the chief teachers and guides of the people. They were distinguished for their adherence to the Law, especially in its ceremonial character. They were equally strict in regard to the rabbinical traditions, and the niceties and sophistries of interpretation which, in the lapse of ages, had grown up in the Jewish schools, and of which the fruits remain to the world in the Talmud. The Pharisees were inveterately hostile to the Roman dominion. Jehovah alone was their king; and it was treason towards Him to acknowledge any other. *His* vicegerent would be the prince Messiah, to whom, therefore, many of them were looking forward, with earnest longing for the great deliverance. Their moral and religious influence could not have been wholly bad, though not of a high character. They paid at least a certain homage to righteousness and to religion, even by their hypocrisy, often alluded to in the New Testament, as well as by their careful attention to times and seasons of prayer and fasting and to other outward observances. It was their tendency to exalt these into an undue prominence, and to substitute form and ceremony for the substance of virtue, while thinking all the time, in their spiritual pride, that they were 'justified' above others by this mere ritualism.

The mass of the people shared largely in the characteristic prejudices of the Pharisees. They were bitterly hostile to their foreign masters, and had the highest opinion of their own righteousness as a nation, and of the inferiority before God of all the nations of the world, in comparison with themselves.* To them alone pertained ' the adoption, and the glory, and the covenants, and the giving of the Law, and the service of God, and the promises.' Last, and greatest of all, from them too was to spring, ' according to the flesh,' the long-expected Christ.†

It is not to be overlooked, in this connection, how great a possession the Jewish people had inherited in the writings of their prophets, in the moral and religious influence which these must have exercised, frequently read as they were in the synagogue services. This rich inheritance was most probably, in one respect, less appreciated than it deserved; the leading or learned classes being too much given to exalt the letter of the Book, and to forget its spirit. And yet we cannot be wrong in saying that, of all the nations then existing in the world, the Jews were the only people among whom that great spiritual Force which we term Christianity could have originated :—no small merit and glory for them, it must be acknowledged, with all their faults. In reference to Jesus himself, it may safely

---

* See how clearly this appears in the words which even the apostle of the Gentiles writes to the converts of Ephesus: Ephes. ii 1-3, 11, 12; comp. Gal. ii. 15.

† Rom. ix. 5. See Appendix, Note B.

be added, that, next to the living communion of his spirit with the Spirit of God, it was to the influence upon his mind of the sacred literature of his people that he was most indebted for the pure and devout feelings of practical goodness and self-renunciation which animated and guided him, from the beginning to the close of his public career.

Turning, in the next place, to the Teacher's words, we learn at once that he addressed himself especially to the people as he found them, assuming and, in some sense, sharing, and also seeking to raise and purify, their ideas on various subjects. What is termed the Sermon on the Mount, though presented to us in the Gospel as a single discourse, is indebted for this form mainly to the pen of the Evangelist. The other synoptists assign many of the sayings included in it to special occasions. We know, too, that Matthew, as indeed the two other narrators, has in some cases placed together in a continuous statement discourses and incidents which had a diverse and separate origin. The native tendency of the evangelical tradition, as at first oral and handed down by memory, would be to arrange and classify in this way. Hence we have a collection of the miracles in chapter ix., and of parables in chapter xiii., and so in some other instances.

The Sermon on the Mount is, nevertheless, an excellent epitome and representative of the whole spirit and substance of our Lord's teaching. The benedictions at the beginning had, most probably, some reference to the Messianic ideas of the day. The people were eager for the coming of the kingdom of heaven, and full of angry zeal and antipathy towards their heathen masters. And they are told that they must prepare for the kingdom by the manifestation of qualities of heart and conduct of a very different kind. The blessed shall be the meek, the upright, the merciful, and the pure in heart. The promised kingdom shall not be theirs, merely because they are Jews, and have been careful about the observances of the Law. 'Good works' which men can see; righteousness greater than that even of their honoured teachers, the Pharisees; tender consideration for the faults of others; brotherly love towards the evil and the good alike; reconciliation with an offended brother rather than gifts upon the altar;—such things as these, summed up in one comprehensive precept, 'All things whatsoever ye would that men should do to you, do ye even so to them,'—such things as these, and not the mere confession, 'Lord, Lord,' are what shall be acceptable to God, and secure admission 'into the kingdom of heaven.'

All this is most admirably said. Can it be surpassed even by the newest and brightest illumination of any modern philosophy? Its lofty and yet practical character is conspicuous—a feature which is apparent throughout this portion of the Master's words, with perhaps one or two exceptions, which shall be presently considered.

When the preacher goes on, in the body of the discourse, to speak of the impartiality and fatherly providence of God, and of the feelings of trust and reverence which men should entertain towards Him, we are introduced, at once, to ideas which we feel to be worthy of our highest veneration. Closely related to them are the exhortations, here and elsewhere, relating to almsgiving, prayer, fasting, forgiveness, and the necessity for obedience as the best evidence of fitness for the heavenly kingdom. And it may be noted what the teacher says on these and the kindred subjects is in obvious harmony with his fundamental conception of the Almighty Being, and of man's relation to Him as that of a child to its parent. A certain resemblance of spiritual nature between man and God is throughout, and most justly, assumed, insomuch that Christ even calls upon his disciples to imitate the Divine excellence, telling them to be perfect even as their Father in heaven is perfect— practical moral goodness being here, again, enforced as the greatest law of human conduct.

The precepts of Christ, it is scarcely necessary to remind the reader, were addressed to a very peculiar state of society. They are, therefore, to be received and applied, in our day, with thought and care, and not blindly. Our modern circumstances are very different from those of the Jews of Palestine, in the year 26 or 27 of the Christian era. Hence, while a principle uttered then may be good and true in itself, the application given to it may not now be equally practicable. In regard, for instance, to almsgiving, — this, it should be remembered, was the long-descended custom of the people. It was also a necessity of the time; for, while there were many poor, there was no public provision for their relief. What then was to be their fate, if they were not to be aided by the free gifts of others? It does not follow that we, in this nineteenth century, and in this country, are to do exactly the same. Nor are we called upon to give up the coat which we ourselves require, any more than to bestow indiscriminate alms; for either course may only tend to demoralize those whom we would benefit. It is only a blind or short-sighted respect for the Gospel which would thus interpret the duties of Christian discipleship.

And yet the *spirit* of such precepts is surely a good and righteous spirit. It tells us not to refuse help where we see it needed. 'Give to him that asketh of thee;' 'lend, hoping for nothing again.' But then, it is carefully added, do not act in this way ostentatiously, 'to be seen of men;' or for any reward which they can give you: 'Let not your left hand know what your right hand doeth.' There is something altogether right and noble in this strain; while yet it may be true that the application in detail of such precepts in our modern life is largely left, and must be left, to the individual judgment. Nor does Jesus anywhere forbid his disciples to combine, with this kindly spirit of his own words, any practical knowledge which the accumulated experience of ages may have put into their hands. This last consideration alone affords an ample reply to any objection which may be urged against these precepts, on the ground of their visionary or their mischievous character. Here, as in other cases, the Christian life does not exact a blind, unreflecting obedience; but rather calls upon us for thought, care, discrimination, in all our conduct.

There is another consideration of much importance to a just estimate of many of these practical teachings of Christ. It is their proverbial character. They are expressed abruptly, with great positiveness, and with a brevity which excludes limitations or conditions. The same character is seen in the moral proverbs of all nations, and it is an element essential to their force and wide acceptance. The moral teacher directs his precept full against the sin or folly which he has in view. Restrictive phrases would deprive it of its power; and these, too, human nature is sure to find out for itself.

It has been noticed that the words of Jesus were spoken to persons who were looking forward to the speedy coming of the 'kingdom of God,' in their own sense of this phrase,—a sense which included the end of the then existing state of the world. How far such ideas were shared by Christ himself may be a question. Without doubt, they have affected and coloured the narratives in which his thoughts have been transmitted to us; and they are expressly attributed to him in various instances.*
This point shall be more fully considered hereafter. It is mentioned here, chiefly because it accounts for the peculiar character of some portions even of the more general teachings of Christ, as they have been handed down to us by his biographers.†

There is a kindred consideration which throws light upon some other expressions. The personal friends who came around Jesus as disciples might be very properly addressed in language which is not wholly applicable to others who never knew him. Does this account for the precepts about not resisting evil? It has often been said that these, in their absolute sense, are inconsistent with human nature, and unfitted for the rough wear and tear of common

* For example, Matt. xvi. 27, 28, xxiv. 29–34. They are not met with in the fourth Gospel, or in the First Epistle of John.

† As Matt. v. 5, xxv. 13, *seq.*; Mark xiii. 32, *seq.*; Luke xiii. 18 *seq.*

life. Granting this, yet (allowing for their proverbial and perhaps somewhat metaphorical form) may not these precepts have been highly suitable in the immediate circumstances in which they were first uttered? Let it be observed, they are really placed before *us* historically, as a part of the *record* of what Christ said to those who were then with him. To us, they make their appeal only in a certain secondary way; and are necessarily subject, as practical principles, to such qualification as reflection, knowledge, time, and circumstance may demand. At all events, it is clear the apostles, going out as they were into the world of that day, would be little likely to win their way by violence of any kind. Concession, in different forms, would be their true policy. Even submission to ill-treatment, in preference to a direct resistance, would be by far the most likely to gain the sympathy of others, and bring them over to the Christian side.

But let us not forget to ask, whether the precepts of non-resistance do not suggest the truest wisdom, in the result, even on the great field of modern life? Those who have, in any degree, carried them out assure us that they do answer, in the long run, in so far as regards the happiness and permanent welfare of those immediately concerned. Inconsistent, then, as such precepts may seem, whether with the teaching of political economy or with the usual practice of the world, we have scarcely a *right* to condemn them;—that is to say, we are not in a position to do so, except on theoretical grounds. It may, in short, be anticipated that, as men become more fully imbued with a just and humane spirit, the more willing and able will they be to embrace even these difficult teachings as, indeed, a true expression of the highest practical wisdom. Nor is it at all unlikely, on the whole, that obedience to them would lead on the great scale to peace among men, to individual prosperity, to the general happiness of communities, at least quite as much as the contrary policy of resistance, retaliation, war, and bloodshed!

In the expressions respecting riches and poverty, it will be thought that there is some degree of harshness and intolerance. Possibly it is so; but have we always the exact words of the Teacher himself? Moreover, it is very possible that we are not in these times sufficiently sensible of the evils of disease and suffering by which, in that age, poverty was often attended, or of the selfishness and the tyrannical spirit which commonly went hand in hand with wealth. For one thing, we have happily no slavery among us, properly so called, with all the miseries and immoralities to which such an institution gives rise. On the other hand—though certainly with poverty and wretchedness around us which do little credit to our civilization—we have many institutions which may be directly ascribed to Christian influences, and which were unknown to the ancient world,—as hospitals, schools of instruction for the blind, places of refuge for the infirm and the aged, reformatories for the young.

Nor is it to be wondered at that Christ, in his intercourse with those around him, often spoke of the poor in terms of sympathy and blessing, or even said that they were peculiarly admissible to the kingdom of heaven; while their richer neighbours in their 'purple and fine linen' could only enter it with difficulty. Such must really have been the relation in which the two classes stood to him. But yet he did not turn away from the rich, or say that they could not be saved. Some of them were probably among his disciples.* In the case of the young man who came to him and asked him what he should do to inherit eternal life, it is related of Jesus that 'he loved him,'† although, at the same time, he assigned him a test of righteousness which made him sorrowful. In the parable of the Talents, it is the man who has received *least* that fails and is punished. Thus, there was evidently no narrow, fanatical preference of poverty above riches, for its own sake.

Such circumstances as these it is but fair to bear

* Luke xix. 2, xxiii. 50; comp. xviii. 25–27.
† Mark x. 21, and parallels.

in mind in judging the language in which Jesus speaks of temporal possessions. It may, in some instances, have been specially addressed and adapted to his immediate auditors, and to circumstances of which we are not well informed. We should remember again, and distinctly, that we reach the mind of Christ only through others who have transmitted to us their distant recollections and impressions of what he said; while these too were, without doubt, in some degree modified by the character of the recipient mind. Nothing of his writing is in our hands, or within our reach. It is most probable, in short, that, if we had more ample materials for judging, we should in this case, as in others, find reason to admire and reverence the wisdom of him who could compel even his adversaries to exclaim, 'Never man spake like this man!'

CHAPTER IV.

FORM AND SUBSTANCE OF OUR LORD'S TEACHING: RELIGIOUS PRINCIPLES.

THE idea of God usually expressed by Christ is that of the Heavenly Father of mankind. This conception was by no means new in the world, but it appears to have been now brought forward with remarkable emphasis and iteration. Moreover, this great idea was presented and exemplified by the Teacher in a way which was equally his own. He not only taught it as a positive doctrine of religion, but so far as we can judge, he lived a life in true accordance with it. He clearly felt it to be, not a mere speculation, but a reality that should influence and rule his conduct; and he shows us, by that final submission which was the triumph and glory of his career, how all-absorbing a truth it was to him.

And the inference from it, 'all ye are brethren,' is equally suggested, equally lofty and practical. We see this in various precepts and parables; as in those which tell us to love our neighbour even as ourselves; to be merciful to one another, as the 'Father also is merciful;' to forgive and do good, striving to imitate Him who maketh his sun to shine and his rain to fall on the evil and the good, the just and the unjust. Great principles these, and calculated to revolutionize the world, if Christian men would only faithfully carry them out in their conduct! This they have never yet done, in any large and persistent way; have never felt themselves able to do. But does this prove that the mind of Him who gave utterance to such thoughts was unpractical and visionary? Rather, may it not reasonably be held, it shows that his ideal was far above that of ordinary men; and that until the Christian nations shall have learnt to follow their Master, even in the acceptance of these ideas, they are not yet worthy of his name?

But yet, let us fairly admit, these great and characteristic conceptions of Jesus have by no means been unfruitful in the world, imperfectly as they have been hitherto embraced. In putting an end to slavery in modern times, surely Christianity has had a very considerable influence, and this it still continues to exercise, with greater or less effect. On this subject, indeed, it does not speak by express precept, but by the silent power of its great principles, the fatherhood of God, the brotherhood of man, with others which are akin to these. The same power is at work in connection with international intercourse, inspiring sympathy and goodwill between nation and nation. The parable of the Good Samaritan is still a lesson for the world, and it is a lesson that has not been given in vain. This was seen not many years ago, when the American people, under the direct prompting of Christian benevolence, sent help to our unemployed operatives, and when the same thing was done, at a more distant period, on even a grander scale, in the case of the Irish peasantry, in their sore distress. It was seen too, in a more striking way still, at the close of the recent war, when the feeling of the English people expressed itself so beneficently towards those who had been their ancient rivals and enemies. Such deeds are of the highest value in every respect; nor can it be questioned that they have been, not indeed originated, but largely stimulated and supported, by the words and the spirit of the Christian Master,—that they have been in a great degree done even 'for Christ's sake.'

Many things, nevertheless, we may rejoice to note, are co-operating to lead us onward to the better manifestation of this good spirit of Christ. Railways, for example, telegraphic communication, commercial and other necessities, are all providentially tending in the one direction, drawing and binding men together in bonds of mutual help and service. But when all such agencies have done their work, and shall have brought the nations to live in peace and brotherhood, we shall then simply have realized the grand ideal of the Christian life virtually set before the world so long ago. Truly, then, we have something still to accomplish, in the way of moral and spiritual progress, before we shall have attained the right proudly to say that we have done with Christ, and can now leave him and his teaching behind us!

The fatherly character which Jesus ascribes to the Unsearchable Being is conspicuous. He is One who sends his blessings on the evil and the good alike. He is One in whose loving kindness we can trust, and who knoweth what we need even before we ask. But He is also a God of justice, who shall judge and reward every man according to his works, expecting from him that hath two talents, or five talents, or one talent, a proportionate result. Yet He is a Being of tender mercy, and ready to forgive; the condition that He lays upon us, while He does so, being that we too forgive those who have injured us. Throughout all that is thus said respecting God, there is nothing to show that He was ever conceived of by Christ as an implacable Being,—in the manner, for example, of the old Grecian mythology; or as one who, for some mysterious reason in his own nature, cannot or will not forgive sinful men, without inflicting the penalty of sin either upon the transgressor, or on some one in his place. In all the words of Jesus, nothing to this effect can be found. On the contrary, the parable of the Prodigal Son not only sets forth the spontaneous and unpurchased mercy of God, but even represents Him under the image of a human father eager to run forward to meet and welcome his returning son. And similarly, Jesus declares, 'there shall be joy in heaven over one sinner that repenteth.'*

It is in the spirit of these representations that he lays so much stress on Love to God as the first commandment, and on Love to our neighbour as the second. 'The God and Father of Jesus Christ' is a Being whom we *can* love. He is just, holy, venerable, in his attributes. Such principles lie at the root, the first of spiritual religion, the second of an upright and useful life. The passages by which these statements may be illustrated, are among the plainest and most

* Compare *infra*, chap. vi.

emphatic in the New Testament. Thus, for example, in the following incident,* one of the Scribes came and asked, 'Which is the first commandment of all? And Jesus answered him, The first of all the commandments is, Hear, O Israel, the Lord our God is one Lord; and thou shalt love the Lord thy God with all thy heart and with all thy soul : .... this is the first commandment. And the second is like, namely this, Thou shalt love thy neighbour as thyself. There is none other commandment greater than these.' The questioner assents, adding, according to Mark, that love to God and our neighbour 'is more than all burnt-offering and sacrifice.' And Jesus then says, 'Thou art not far from the kingdom of God.' This language is at one with some kindred expressions in the fourth Gospel, in which the true test of discipleship is said to be precisely in the love which we bear to one another : 'By this shall all men know that ye are my disciples, if ye have love one to another.'†

In such words as these there is a marvellous simplicity and power. And another thing is equally clear. It is the entire freedom of such language from those peculiar dogmatic statements which have usually been the burden of theological creeds; which, in

---

* Mark xii. 28-34; compare the parallels.
† John xiii. 34, 35. See an admirable Sermon of Dean Stanley's, on the 'Eleventh Commandment,' forming the introduction to his *Lectures on the Church of Scotland*.

this form, have so constantly tended and still tend, to destroy the unity and peace of Christendom; and which have often proved the means, direct or indirect, of bringing good men to the stake.

While this is said, it should not be overlooked that Christ does not fail to give us an example which is wholly favourable to the exercise of mental freedom. He does not speak as though he expected his followers, for all time to come, to yield a blind or unquestioning assent even to his own words. He constantly reasons with those who come to him, and evidently intended to work in their minds a rational, individual conviction. He thus appears as one who desired to encourage intellectual activity, and the love of truth for its own sake. He himself resisted the implied claims of the Pharisees to obedience; he reproved their hypocrisy in the strongest language; and he disregarded their requirements about sabbath-keeping, and other formalities. He said expressly, on one occasion, 'Why judge ye not of yourselves what is right?'*—words from which we can only make one inference, and that is manifestly in favour of mental liberty. In this the Master was well followed by his apostle, Paul, who specially exhorts his friends to 'stand fast in the liberty wherewith Christ hath made us free,'† and who applied this great principle boldly and at once to the most practical question of his own day,

* Luke xii. 57. † Gal. v. 1.

that of the authority of the Law over Gentile converts. In these respects, as before, the Christian life, as exemplified by Christ, would not fail, if truly followed, to lead to great and admirable results in human society. He, we may be sure, would have promptly rejected the idea of an infallible Pope, equally with that of an infallible Protestant Church!

Closely related to the idea of God is the estimate which is formed of human nature. As usually depicted by theologians of various schools, man is a being depraved by original sin, the bondman of Satan, and deserving of eternal perdition. But human nature is never so represented by Christ. Men, indeed, he regards as exposed to the subtle attacks of the Evil One; but this diabolical power is hostile to them. It is not congenial, or naturally acceptable; and if they are liable to temptation and sin, yet they are also capable of penitence, of a return of virtue, and to good resolutions and actions. Jesus himself came, he declares, 'to call sinners to repentance;' and he shows us clearly that he considered lost and sinful man as possessed of the capacity to approach nearer and nearer even to the Infinite perfection. Thus, in his estimation, sin and the miseries which result from it are *not* man's natural state. They are the working of a strange and demoniacal power, the enemy alike of God and man. They are a disease, something like the bodily diseases by which men are afflicted, and capable of being expelled by the physician of souls. Naturally, men are the 'children' of God. Jesus constantly speaks of them as having that character, as, conversely, he everywhere represents the Almighty Being as our common Father in heaven. When they brought young children to him, he not only took them up in his arms and blessed them, but added the significant words, 'of such is the kingdom of heaven.' In the absolute sense of the word, it is true, 'none is *good* but one, even God;' and the teacher deprecates and disclaims the epithet 'good' even for himself.* In comparison, therefore, with Him who alone is the Good and Righteous, every man is imperfect and sinful. But there are degrees, even in this; some are worse than others, as some are better; and all that Christ says on this subject, or suggests, corresponds, in short, in an eminent degree, to our usual experience and observation of human life.

The important subject of retribution for sin is one of which he not unfrequently speaks. It is brought before us under various figures, such as beating with many stripes, or with few according to desert; casting into the outer darkness; burning in a furnace of fire; cutting asunder; casting into Gehenna.† The

---

* Mark x. 18.

† See Luke xii. 5, 46–48; comp. Matt. v. 29, 30, xiii. 40–42, xxv. 41, *seq.*

essential idea thus conveyed is, that wilful wrongdoing, wilful sin, shall be followed by its just punishment. The experience of human life verifies the principle; showing us that Christ, in these declarations, spoke like a prophet of the truth. But it is clear that the expressions in which this great principle is embodied are derived, as in other cases, from the popular ideas of the time. This would appear to be especially the case in those passages which, in two (only) of the Gospels,* speak of 'eternal fire.' Strictly read, these words are 'age-enduring fire.' But not to insist upon this, the phrase is capable of a satisfactory explanation, without admitting that terrible article of the popular belief which would change the Almighty Parent into the tyrant of the universe, into One who consigns countless myriads of his own creatures, not to mere annihilation, but to an existence of un-

* Matt. xviii. 8, xxv. 41, 46; parallel to these is Mark ix. 43–46; but here verses 44, 46, are interpolations, as well as the final words of v. 45, 'into the unquenchable fire.' (See Dean Alford's *New Testament Revised*.) It is especially to be noted that the epithet 'eternal,' in connection with this subject, occurs only in the above three instances—the passage in Mark ix. being the *same* as Matt. xviii. 8. Paul, Luke, and John, never speak of eternal fire, though often referring to the life eternal. So little true is the statement, made by the late Archbishop Longley, that the scriptural evidence for the eternal suffering of the lost is equally 'sure' with that for the belief in the eternal happiness of the saved. (*Pastoral Letter*, 1864.)

ending torment,—representing Him even as keeping them alive, and not allowing them to die, in order that they may be in suffering for ever. It cannot be, it is not for a moment to be thought, that Jesus Christ really intended to teach such a doctrine as this, and a reasonable interpretation of his expressions relieves them, and relieves Christianity of all this horror.

The two words in the New Testament rendered by 'hell' are the words *Gehenna* and *hades*, the latter a well-known term denoting simply the *unseen state*. Gehenna is a proper name,* belonging originally to the valley of Hinnom, near Jerusalem. This was long an abominable place to the ancient Jew, as having been the scene of idolatrous rites and the immolation of human victims to a heathen god. It was a spot, in Christ's time, where the entrance was supposed to be to the region of future punishment, and where, there is reason to believe, fires were continually burning † to consume the refuse from the city there thrown. Such was the character of the spot and its associations *long before* the time of Christ, who, in his usual manner, makes use of the established phraseology connected with the place, and denotes by its

---

* It is treated as such by the ancient versions, not being translated.

† This is alluded to in the phrase *eternal* fire. See Schleusner, *Lex.* in *N. T.*; also Grimm, *Lex. N. T.*, both in the word Γεεννα.

evil name the scene of future punishment. This, it must be evident, he does in a popular sense, simply. He adopts words and ideas already current among his people to express retribution for sin, in order to convey to them his own thoughts on the same subject.* Nothing could be more natural or more inevitable. But popular phrases, thus used, are not to be accepted with a kind of legal strictness, or so interpreted as to contradict both the whole tenor of the Christian teaching and the persistent intimations of human nature respecting the merciful and gracious character of the Almighty; nor should this one figure of burning in fire be selected and made prominent above the other figures which, as before pointed out, are also used to denote the same idea of just retribution under different forms of expression.†

We may then fairly exculpate our Lord, and exonerate Christianity, from the intolerable imputation of teaching, as a permanent element of religion, anything so dreadful, and so repulsive to all our better ideas of

---

* It is impossible in this connection to overlook the fact that the whole of the New Testament language respecting the future destiny of the wicked is found in the Book of Enoch,— a work which was known to the writer of the Epistle of Jude, and which is probably older than any of our Gospels. See Bishop Colenso on the Pentateuch, Part III.; also Dillmann's *Buch Henoch*, Kap. 27. also p. 131-2; and compare the article on the subject in Dr. Wm. Smith's Dictionary of the Bible.

† The reader may compare Dr. Pusey's Sermon in defence of this doctrine (1864).

God, as the common doctrine of eternal punishment. There can be little doubt that the Christian world, in all its sections, will, in time, come to see, and be glad to believe, that such is the case. Meantime, it is well if the old and widely prevalent idea of hell-fire shall, by any possibility, have tended to the greater righteousness of those who profess to hold it. Judging from the present moral condition of multitudes in our own and in other Christian lands, it is hard to think that such has been its true influence. The unjust and cruel character of the doctrine is more or less felt even by those who receive it; and this fact cannot but undermine its power,—preventing it, in effect, from exercising any high or ennobling influence, or from acting even as a deterring check and safeguard, amidst the temptations of life.

It will not be possible, in this brief summary of the teachings of Jesus, to attempt to enter upon all the topics which such a theme suggests. It may be enough to recall how tender and considerate he was towards the poor and the sinful; how intolerant to the exaggerated pharisaism and ceremonialism of his day; how he constantly sets himself against such things as formal sabbath observance, and other kinds of mere outward ritualism, as it prevailed in his own time. In all this, he well shows us that rites and ceremonies are insufficient in themselves to secure the favour of the great Observer and Judge, however serviceable they may be as aids or stimulants to the faith and devotion of certain classes of persons. 'Mercy and not sacrifice' was the burden of his teaching on such subjects; nor does he ever lose sight of his own most fruitful principle, that practically to do the will of God, in the common daily work of life, and not the mere saying of creeds, is the one indispensable condition of the Divine blessing.*

The subject of Prayer belongs to the present connection. The teaching of Jesus in reference to it is deserving of especial consideration in the midst of the discussions of our own time. He exhorts his followers, indeed, to pray—rightly and wisely recognizing the need of private communion between the spirit of man and the Spirit of God, the importance of our voluntary and conscious seeking to draw near and bow down, especially in secret prayer, before the Infinite Father. But yet, it is evident that Christ places submission to the Divine Will among the foremost of his precepts. This is so conspicuous in the principal passage on the subject, that it is reasonable, in one or two other cases,† to infer that the form of the narrative must be mainly due to the mind of the narrator. The most express example of a prayer of Christ's preserved in the three synoptics contains

---

* Comp. Mark iii. 31-35; Luke viii. 19-21; Matt vii. 21, *seq.*

† Luke xi. 8, xviii. 5.

but one request for material good. This again, is restricted to the simplest and most pressing of our wants, 'daily bread;' the very use of such words being, in truth, an expression of dependence; while all the rest of the prayer may be understood of spiritual requests alone. There is perfect submission, too, side by side even with this request; 'Thy will be done.' And how naturally and beautifully the same spirit of Christ is manifested in his own prayer in Gethsemane, where we see the most earnest entreaty accompanied by the most absolute resignation.

On one particular in the Lord's Prayer an especial stress is laid, showing us afresh the self-restraining and practical character of the righteousness which Christ desired in his followers. 'If ye forgive men their trespasses, your heavenly Father will also forgive you. But if ye forgive not men their trespasses, neither will your Father forgive your trespasses.' This may seem poor and commonplace by the side of the subtleties of ancient or modern theology—about the efficacy of baptism, faith, atonement, confession, sacramental observances. It may seem but poor and commonplace, yet it is unquestionably Christian; and one who would follow Christ, and live the Christian life, will do well not to forget this. Perhaps, too, he will find, in the perplexities and trials of actual experience, that it is not really any too light or easy task, or test of obedience, that is thus put upon him;

as undoubtedly he will find that a faithful obedience is the surest path to the conscious peace and blessing of the upright soul.

There is one objection of which it will be proper to take notice here. The thoughts expressed by Christ in reference to God, and man's relations to Him, are to a great degree *anthropomorphic*, or they directly imply conceptions which are so. But how, it may be asked, could the speaker have addressed the people of his time in any other language? Nay, at this moment, amidst the advanced scientific knowledge of our day, can even the most cultivated human intelligence form any conception of the Infinite Spirit which shall be calculated to impress the minds of ordinary people, without largely assuming and implying the 'personality' of God, even as Christ did? Is it not perfectly reasonable, too, that in speaking of that inscrutable Creative Power which, as a personal existence, no man hath seen or can see, we should affirm its possession of attributes, moral and intellectual, corresponding with, though far transcending, those which we are conscious of possessing ourselves? We may be very sure that He in whom 'we live and move and have our being,' is in no way inferior to us, His children, in any good gift or power of which we are able to conceive. Unless we keep this steadily in view, the idea of God will be in danger of being refined away until it become a mere vague and powerless sentiment of we know not what. This is everywhere, as if by a natural and unconscious instinct, avoided by the Teacher; and so it was by those who took up his work after him, and handed down his influence to succeeding generations. It was so in his case, it is plain, not only because it was the long-descended habit of his people thus definitely and strongly to think and speak of God, but even because he himself deeply felt the great reality of the Divine Presence, and the immediate conscious influence of the Divine Spirit within his own heart.

CHAPTER V.

THE FINAL SCENES.

The ministry of Christ was rapidly drawing to its close at the approach of the Passover of the year 27, A.D., the year following that in which he first attracted attention as a teacher.* Some of the incidents by which the last days were marked are among the most touching and suggestive in his brief career.

The entry into Jerusalem was a short interlude of popularity and triumph, serving by the contrast to

* This statement rests on the assumption (which is as probable as any other) that the ministry comprised only one whole year and part of another.

set off and illustrate what was to follow. Jesus, it would appear, now permitted the people openly to salute him as the Christ, whereas, according to the synoptical narratives, he had previously shrunk from assuming this title. They shouted, 'Hosanna to the Son of David.' It will be observed that we have no explanation of the sense in which he thus allowed himself to be acknowledged in that great character. Much in his own words may show us that it could not have been in any low or political sense. Throughout the narrative of the three Gospels we can see that he had thoughts of his own of a kingdom not of this world; a kingdom in which the divine qualities he had pronounced 'blessed' should be the ruling characteristics of his disciples.

He had repelled the suggestion which had offered him 'the kingdoms of the world and the glory of them,' with words implying his own self-devotion to the service of God alone. He had said expressly, 'the kingdom of God cometh not with observation,' for that it is a kingdom not of the outward and palpable kind, but inward and spiritual. He had never shown himself disposed to external and sensational display, but was always conspicuously natural and unaffected in his words and actions.

It is but fair, therefore, to understand this assumption of the Messianic title, in the highest sense which the act and the words referring to it will reasonably bear—knowing, as we do, that those who have recorded words and incidents for us would only interpret them through the medium of their own imperfect conceptions.* Long after his death, these had not lost their power, for the disciples still anticipated their Master's return to the earth, then at last to enter upon his temporal kingdom. Probably we have in such considerations the true explanation of any inconsistency which may appear on the face of the narratives, in the various expressions of Jesus respecting his own position. His thoughts, as formerly observed, have been transmitted to us through the colouring medium of other minds; while those who have written of him had themselves to learn, by the prolonged discipline of many years and of disappointed hopes, that he should reign as Christ, not on earth, but in heaven; and not in their sense, but in the most lofty and spiritual sense of that expression. This higher knowledge had doubtless been acquired by the fourth Evangelist, more than by the synoptists. He never speaks as they do of the Second Advent, in the primitive Judaic sense of the idea; and he had learnt to think of the universality and spirituality of the kingdom of God among men, in a way which had not yet become familiar to

* In illustration, See Matt. xvi. 21-23, xx. 20-27; Luke xxii. 24-30, xxiv. 21; Mark x. 35-45.

the earlier Evangelists, or even perhaps to the mind of St. Paul himself.*

But this higher conception by Jesus of the great work of his life necessarily involved the thought of his own destruction. The continued diffusion of his spiritual influence in the world required that he should cease to live; for, as a Jew, he was shut up within the laws and customs of his own people; and these were of so narrow and exclusive a character as to make it impossible for him during his lifetime to receive as disciples the people of other and heathen races.† Hence the necessity for his death, and this was easily brought about. On the one hand, his adversaries, the Pharisees, were ready to accuse him before the Roman tribunal of political ambition; on the other hand, the people, speedily disappointed and embittered by his non-fulfilment of the temporal hopes which they had founded upon him, allowed their leaders to work their will, and themselves shouted for his crucifixion.

With this prospect immediately in sight and doubtless well understood, Jesus was ever calm and firm, prepared to meet the great trial which was so surely awaiting him. And thus he has taught the world, by the express lesson of his own high example,

* At least in his earlier Epistles; see 1 and 2 Thess. *passim*, and comp. 1 Cor. xv. 50-53; Philip. iii. 20.

† See this more fully set forth in the next chapter.

that self-sacrifice—the giving up of something which you value for the sake of God or man—is an essential element of Christian obedience; that it is an acceptable offering to the God of truth and right; and that he who would follow Christ with the faith of true discipleship must be willing and prepared, if needs be, even to lay down life itself at the call of sacred duty.

Of the later incidents, one of the most interesting, and one, at the same time, the most important in its after-influence and consequences, was the Passover Supper, taken by the Master along with his disciples the evening before his death. The meal was the ordinary meal proper to the occasion. It was eaten, so far as can be learnt, in the usual manner. The three synoptists vary somewhat from each other in their account of the words employed in the closing incident. They write in evident unconsciousness of the momentous consequences which are to result from what they tell. But they all speak of the broken bread, and of the wine poured out, as significant of the body that was slain and the blood that was shed for others. The definite import of these expressions is nowhere recorded for us, and must consequently be gathered by interpretation from the known results of the death of Christ,* as these appear in the New Testament. It is easy, however,

* See *infra*, Chapter VI.

to see that the words employed at least convey the same idea of self-sacrifice which appears in other instances. Luke alone of the Evangelists records the commemorative nature of the rite: 'Do this in remembrance of me.' In this point he is carefully followed by St. Paul—or rather, it should be said, he follows the longer account of that apostle—for there can be little doubt the Gospel narrative is the later in the order of time.* From the primitive history of the institution it is clear that it was appointed, in the conception of the Evangelists, with the simple memorial purpose of celebrating the death of Christ, and perpetuating the anticipation of his second coming.

The sacrificial and mystical ideas which are now so strangely acceptable to many persons, were an aftergrowth, easily traceable to the credulous and ill-informed faith of subsequent generations. Within the New Testament such ideas are not to be found. In its pages the rite is a simple commemoration. And such it may still be;—while yet symbolical, not only of the love and veneration with which the disciple looks back upon the memory of his departed Master, but also of the living hope and aspiration which he cherishes for union with Him hereafter, in his glorified and heavenly state.

The scene in Gethsemane speedily followed. It

* 1 Cor. xi. 24-20; Luke xxii. 19.

is full of instruction and of deep sorrowful interest. Jesus manifestly *felt* the trial to which he was called; felt it to be one that would task his utmost strength. His was a nature of almost feminine tenderness, susceptible, we may not doubt, of every genuine human emotion. Though brave and unflinching in the path of duty, this, we can plainly see, did not arise from insensibility. Hence those words of earnest, agonizing prayer. For a moment he shrank from the trial, and desired that the cup might pass from him—' O my Father, if it be possible, let this cup pass from me.' But this outburst of natural feeling was only transient. It speedily passed, although the words were repeated three times, showing us that the emotion was deep and not momentary. Moreover, its existence was a necessary condition and prelude to the peace and triumph which ensued, giving, as it did, their full and most touching import to the words, ' not as I will, but as thou wilt.'* Here was perfect self-surrender

---

* The writer may mention an illustrative incident. He was present at the service in York Minster on the evening of Good Friday last (1874). The sermon was on the death of Christ, and delivered by the celebrated Ritualistic preacher, the Rev. George Body. He dwelt with special emphasis upon the free, voluntary, 'willing' character of the death, the 'sacrifice,' of Christ. But he left entirely out of sight the scene in Gethsemane—the prayer of Jesus that the cup might pass from him, if it were possible. Was this omission intentional, or was it only an oversight of negligence? In either case, on

again; fortitude, trust, submission, in circumstances of the deepest woe, and such as must ever command the sympathy and admiration of thoughtful men.

The charge upon which Jesus was arraigned and condemned was that of saying that he himself was 'Christ, a king.'* All the Evangelists agree in this. His claim was construed to be blasphemous, and this character it would doubtless wear to unsympathizing spectators. The charge against him was so framed also as to be equivalent to an accusation of treason against the Romans. Claiming to be *Christ*, or even being supposed to do so, it would easily be made to appear to their eyes that the accused man had a political object, and was possessed of a dangerous influence among the people. Accordingly, the inscription which Pilate put over his cross, announced him to the world as 'Jesus of Nazareth, the king of the Jews.'

We are told by one Evangelist that, at first, his accusers were at a loss to find witnesses against him,† till at length they found two who falsely accused him of having spoken in a certain way against the *temple*. So little, be it observed, did it enter into

such an occasion, in such a connection, the omission is significant. It exemplifies the prevailing popular tendency, conscious or unconscious, to subordinate the truth of Scripture to theological system and sect.

* Luke xxiii. 2, and compare the parallels.
† Matt. xxvi. 59–63.

their thoughts to charge him with the highest blasphemy of all, as they would consider it, that of having said that he was GOD! And yet, to a Jew, who would not even pronounce the Holy Name, nor permit any graven image or other representation of the Invisible to be made, the latter charge would have been the heaviest that could have been brought had it been possible to make it. The inference is at once suggested, that it was not within their power to bring forward such an accusation; that the utmost which they could allege against their victim was, that he was guilty of having pretended to be the Christ—the Son of God.* This was enough for their purpose. From the Jewish point of view it was blasphemy, as they chose to say; from the Roman, it was treason against Cæsar.

The trial, if such it may be termed, was soon at an end, and summary justice, or injustice, was the custom of the time. The dreadful process of crucifixion speedily followed; but even on the cross, the calmness, the moral strength and dignity of brighter days did not abandon the sufferer. It may be that passing feelings of despair found utterance in the words which he repeated from the twenty-second Psalm. But it is not undeserving of notice that those words are introductory in the Psalm to a

---

* On this epithet see the Appendix, Note E.

burst of religious trust and exultation.* We know that he said at last, 'Father, into Thy hands I commend my spirit;' and how could he feel, therefore, that God had forsaken him? The exclamation should probably be taken as indicative of the peace and triumph with which the sufferer fulfilled his Father's will, and finally drank, even to the dregs, the bitter cup which could not pass from him.

And not only this. A greater proof of the tranquil and holy devoutness of his spirit was yet to come, when he breathed forth the prayer, 'Father, forgive them; they know not what they do.'† We do not wonder that the centurion, when he saw what was done, 'glorified God, saying, Certainly this was a righteous man.'

It is impossible to read the narratives of this memorable scene without observing a circumstance of the utmost significance. It is, that they contain no allusion whatever to what so many now suppose to have been the true meaning and purpose of the transaction. Jesus upon the cross was, indeed, no ordinary person, suffering the penalty of a fearful death for crimes of blasphemy and treason which he had not committed. Far from this. But neither is this, as

---

* Ps. xxii. 22, *seq.*

† Luke xxiii. 34. The words are only given by St. Luke, and it is proper to notice that some ancient authorities are without them. But Tischendorf admits them. They are in perfect keeping with the general spirit of Christ's teaching.

we are usually told, what the Scripture really contains. It is something infinitely greater. The sufferer, who prays in his agony that the cup may pass from him, who calls upon his God, and asks the Divine forgiveness for his murderers, who commends his spirit into the hands of his Father in heaven, and meekly bows his head and dies—this is the ALMIGHTY BEING himself, mocked and buffeted and spit upon by sinful men, lifted up and nailed by them to the cross and crucified, like any common malefactor of the day—but the Evangelists pass coldly over this marvellous fact, without the slightest allusion to it!

Nor is this all; for, in thus suffering and dying, Christ is making an atonement and expiation of unspeakable value, affecting the whole race of men for all ages to come. In the words of the Second Article of the English Church, he is dying ' to reconcile his Father to us, and to be a sacrifice, not only for original guilt, but also for actual sins of men.' He is dying, we are told, in various phrase, to satisfy the demands of the infinite justice, which but for this sacrifice and propitiation must have consigned the human race to endless misery in hell. Such is the *true* character of that scene; but then the Evangelists, all four, in describing what takes place, leave this out of sight! It is true, they introduce many small incidents which are of no importance whatever, and which were hardly worth mentioning, except that they give life and character to their descriptions. But they do not suggest to their readers, even by a slight hint or a passing allusion, the true significance or the true effect of what was being done. Were they, then, themselves in ignorance of it? Or could they wish their readers to be ignorant? Or were they only careless and forgetful, while yet the transaction was of infinite weight and value in the sight of God? They were writing forty years or more after the event. Is it, then, to be supposed that the true character of what took place had faded from their thoughts?

How differently, at all events, a narrator under modern prepossessions can treat the subject may be illustrated by a single sentence. M. de Pressensé in a recent work, in speaking of the siege of Jerusalem, observes of that terrible time, that Josephus knew not that Jerusalem was then expiating a yet darker crime than one he had just mentioned, 'and that its soil, once sacred, had been stained by the *blood of God*.'* The Evangelists have no remark of this kind to make; they utter no word to lead us to think that it was 'the blood of God' that was being shed; not a word to indicate that such an idea (so gross and heathenish as it is) had ever entered, or could enter, into their minds.† Not a word to

* Pressensé. *Early Years of Christianity*, p. 364.
† On Acts xx. 28, see the Appendix, Note C.

this effect, but very much to the contrary. Strange inconsistency, again, between the popular theologies of the nineteenth century and the New Testament.

Finally, Jesus upon the cross, meekly bowing his head to die, willing to die, because even such was the heavenly Father's decree, praying for the forgiveness of his enemies, and committing his spirit in peace to the Almighty keeping,—Jesus, as he is thus set before us by the Evangelists, was and is an example to the world for all ages to come. He was so, however, and he is so, only on the supposition that he was truly what he appeared to be, what he is termed by an apostolical writer, even one of many 'brethren,' 'made perfect' by the sufferings through which he was called to pass.* If he were not this, if he were a human being in outward appearance only, if he were not a man in reality, but God himself, surely he is no example for *us* in any true sense of the word, and he cannot be so. For, in that case, could we think that the humiliation, agony, submission to pain and woe, were real? *Could* they be real, and not a mere passing show, put on for the occasion? What moral strength or comfort could frail and tempted man derive from the spectacle of an Infinite Being called to suffer, pretending to suffer, as Jesus did? The whole idea of this seems to be so remote from possibility, and so contrary to

* Heb. ii. 10-18; v. 7-9.

every dictate of natural common sense, that the thoughtful mind instinctively revolts from it, and is only made to receive it by the constraining force of habit and education. Without doubt, the conception referred to is slowly crumbling away. It is ceasing, and it must cease, to have authority or influence among reasonable men. May the religious guides of our people be wise in time; and, before it is too late, show them how to replace old and worn-out theories of patristic and mediæval superstition with the pure, natural, invigorating doctrine of Jesus Christ!

CHAPTER VI.

THE ATONEMENT OR RECONCILIATION BY THE DEATH OF CHRIST.

THE omission and silence referred to in the last chapter may be accounted for. We have seen that the oldest part of the New Testament is the Pauline Epistles. At the time when these were written, the troublesome question about the claims of the Law and the relation of the Gentiles to the Gospel was still the subject of earnest discussion, as appears from the Epistles to the Galatians, the Romans, the Ephesians and the Colossians. At an interval of from twenty to thirty years afterwards, the earliest date to which the Gospels can be referred, always excepting the fourth, which is still later, the controversy alluded to had been virtually settled, and decided in favour of the Gentiles. Hence, although the *death* of the Messiah had afforded the great means for its termination, yet when the narratives of the crucifixion were composed there was no occasion to refer either to a controversy which had originated only after that event, or to the arguments and circumstances by which it had been closed. The whole question was now simply a thing of the past, and it does not, therefore, recur prominently either in the Gospels, or in the later writings of the New Testament, except in the form of occasional allusions to the death of Christ, under images derived from the Levitical sacrifices.*

This will be really understood from a brief exposition of the circumstances and arguments just referred to.

The Jewish people, it would appear, had not expected the death of the Messiah. It might well, indeed, be a strange and unnatural idea to their minds, that the long expected Prince, the specially beloved 'Son of God,' should be rejected by his own people, and destroyed at the hands of triumphant enemies. Jesus, however, must himself have distinctly foreseen his approaching sufferings and death. On several occasions he spoke of them to the disciples; but they, we are told, 'understood none of

* See the note at the end of this chapter.

these things.' On one occasion Peter expressly said, 'Be it far from thee, Lord; this shall not be unto thee.'* At the crucifixion, 'all the disciples forsook him and fled.' The event fell with sudden and overwhelming terror upon their unprepared minds; as, indeed, according to the narratives, they were equally unprepared for the resurrection.

But, as we have seen, the death of Christ was inevitable under the circumstances. We can now also see that it was a *necessary* part of the whole scheme of divine Providence, and this for two principal reasons: first, to check, if it could not entirely destroy, the vain hopes of temporal power and conquest which evidently filled the minds of the early disciples. The crucifixion would at least make it very plain to them that such hopes could have no immediate fulfilment in connection with their Master. But, secondly, what proved to be of the most durable importance, the same event was needed for the extension of the Gospel beyond the limits of the Hebrew nation to the Gentile world. This statement requires a more particular elucidation.

By his birth, Jesus Christ was a Jew, and 'under the Law.' He did not address himself, in his own ministry, to any except 'the lost sheep of the house

* Matt. xvi. 21-23; comp. Luke ix. 45; xviii. 31-34; John xii. 34.

of Israel.'* Yet he knew, nevertheless, that he had 'other sheep, which were not of that fold.'† The strong prejudices of the people, however, could not readily believe that others besides Jews should be admitted to come in and share with them the anticipated glories and blessings of the kingdom of heaven. This feeling appears at times very strongly, especially among the stricter Judaizing zealots and Pharisees. Several passages in the book of Acts show us this, and also how great was the opposition which Paul encountered, in his determination to preach the Gospel to the Gentiles. The conservative position was, that none but Jews 'by nature,' or by 'conversion,' could be permitted to be subjects of Christ; and it was held that no Gentile could become a Christian without first submitting to certain Mosaic rites, or in fact embracing Judaism.‡

Had this party prevailed, there would have been an end to the spirituality and universality of the Gospel. Christianity would have been simply a 'heresy' of Judaism. It would have lost its interest for the world; and, most probably, it would not have survived the century which gave it birth. But the free-minded and outspoken Paul, by his preaching and his writings, prevented this abortive result, although some even of the most influential of his

---

* Comp. Matt. xv. 21, *seq.* † John x. 16; comp. xii. 24.
‡ Acts x.; xv. 3, 5; comp. xxii. 21, 22; Gal. ii. 7, *seq.*

Christian contemporaries hindered him in his work, and did what they could to withstand his influence.*

The death of the Messiah was the one great channel through which the extension of Christianity to the world was brought about. In other, and more scriptural phrase, it was by that event that the 'wall of partition' between Jew and Gentile was thrown down, and the 'atonement,' or 'reconciliation' of man to God, was effected.†

But let us carefully observe the true import of such expressions. The 'reconciliation' referred to is nowhere said to have been that of God to man; nowhere in the New Testament. This is only an idea of later times, common indeed in the dogmatic teaching of our own day, but altogether absent from the New Testament. The reconciliation meant was that of sinful and alienated man to the merciful God. The necessity for it, and for the particular form which it assumed, was, to the Jewish mind, founded upon certain circumstances and ideas which must be now briefly enumerated.

The Jews had learnt to esteem themselves as the righteous and favourite people of God. The Gentiles were sinners and outcasts in His sight. The latter could not be received by the Messiah, for He belonged exclusively to the privileged race of Abra-

---

* Gal. ii.; Acts xviii. 5, 6; xxii. 21-23.
† Rom. v. 10, 11; 1 Cor. v. 17, *seq.*

ham—so, by the latter, it was believed. But then the Jews, when they rejected and crucified the Christ, cut themselves off by their own deed from that national prerogative of theirs. He, by his death, ceased to be a man under their law, and, rising to heaven, he became a spiritual being. How, then, is he now to be approached and received? Simply, for Jew and Gentile alike, through *faith*, belief in him in his risen and glorified state.* The Jew, with all the strictness of his notions about the righteousness of the law, was not really righteous, for he had not been able to keep the law.† If justice were done, he too must be cast out of the promised kingdom; but God was merciful to Jew and Gentile alike. Through the death of his 'Son,' the Messiah, He made known 'the riches of his grace' to the world,‡ and allowed an end to be put to the disqualification caused to all alike by the want of righteousness. 'Rich in mercy,' He did this for the Jew; as he did it also for the Gentile. Those who were 'baptized into Jesus Christ were baptized into his death;' and, rising again with him to the new life of faith, they were now dead to the law, and released from its claims.§ The way of access for all was *faith;* and faith was now to be reckoned for the righteousness‖ in which the Jew was so ready to

---

* Rom. x. 9; iii. 22, seq., v. 1, seq.   † Rom. ii., iii.
‡ Ephes. ii. 4–13.   § Rom. vi. 3, seq.   ‖ Rom. iv.

glory as his exclusive possession, but which he did not really possess. It would equally be accounted for righteousness to the Gentile, so that his want of the legality of the Jew should be no effectual bar to discipleship in the sight of God. Was He 'the God of the Jews only? Was he not also of the Gentiles? Yes, of the Gentiles also.' 'Circumcision' and 'uncircumcision' He alike justifies (or accounts righteous) 'through faith.'*

By his *death*, therefore, the Messiah became the spiritual head of the universal church, and access to Him was thus opened to all men, graciously offered to 'all,' by the free gift of God. It was easy, then, and almost literally exact, to say that he 'died for' those who thus became admissible, by his dying, within the fold of his people, in spite of their past sins. There was but little of metaphor in the words when it was declared that he 'shed his blood' and 'laid down his life' and 'gave himself' *for* others.

Again, it was inevitable that a Jewish writer should in such a case adopt phraseology derived from the usages of his own ancient religion, and should speak of Jesus, in his death, as a 'sacrifice;' even as being 'set forth to be a propitiation.'† In such

---

* Rom. iii. 29, 30.

† Rom. iii. 25. The rendering should most probably be, whom God hath set forth to be a propitiation in his blood

expressions there is something of figure; but the literal fact which the figure conveys is *not* that the merciful Father of all needed to be appeased by the death of an innocent victim,—much as an ancient Greek might have thought of Jupiter or Neptune. Nor was it that the infinite justice and holiness of God required 'satisfaction,' and must obtain this even by the immolation of an innocent victim. It was not *this*,—at least this is nowhere laid down, or directly conveyed, in the New Testament. It was not this, therefore, but simply that the earthly and mortal Christ through his death ascended his spiritual throne, became the heavenly and glorified Christ in whom all things have been created anew;* and is now accessible to all men alike, over all the world, by the simple faith and obedience of discipleship, without regard to Jewish rites, or, in other words, 'without the deeds of the law.'

It is necessary, however, to observe more particularly what it was that constituted the equal disqualification of all for immediate admission to the privileges of discipleship. It was the *sins* of all. 'None were righteous, no not one;' all were 'concluded under sin.' But the acknowledgment of the Messiah, 'by faith,' that is, the acceptance of

---

through faith.'—So Prof. Jowett, Meyer, De Wette, Bunsen's *Bibelwerk*, and others of the highest authority.

* Compare Ephes. i.; Coloss. i.

Jesus of Nazareth as the promised Christ,* with the practical obedience which this naturally involved, was allowed, by the mercy of God, to confer the needed righteousness and consequent admission to the Messiah's kingdom. Such was the conception and such the argument maintained by Paul against the Judaizers of his day. Hence, again, it was an obvious thing to say, that Christ 'died for sin,' the 'just for the unjust,' that he 'gave his life a ransom for many;'—figurative expressions, it is plain, derived from the ancient sacrifices and their connected ideas. It was not, I repeat, that the infinite justice, or the infinite wrath, would have consigned sinful men to everlasting suffering, in punishment of their transgressions: this is *nowhere* stated in the pages of the New Testament, but is only the speculative, theological solution of a supposed difficulty. It is nowhere *stated* within the New Testament, as the reader may see who will take the trouble to look there for himself. Nor are we anywhere *told* that Jesus Christ, being an infinite person, was able, by sacrificing himself, to make an infinite atonement for the sins of the world, and so to release men from well-deserved damnation. And indeed, if this be the doctrine of any creed, if it be really held by any Christian of modern times, as it

---

* Compare such passages as John iv. 26; viii. 24, 28; xi. 27, xiii. 19; Acts ix. 20–22; xviii. 28; 1 John v. 1, 5.

would seem to be by some.* is it not manifestly untrue? For is not sin still punished? Do those who profess the old doctrines of propitiation and substitution, think that hell has ceased to exist? And, if it has not, how shall any one affirm that Christ, by his death, has redeemed and saved a sinful world from the miserable consequences of transgression? Clearly, on the popular theory, those consequences still follow, still await the sinner, and innumerable millions of sinful men are yearly consigned to the unspeakable torments of hell, quite as much as if Christ had never lived. What then, again, I would ask, is the popular theory worth?

The peculiar scriptural language to which I am referring is, therefore, in truth easily explicable, with a reasonable degree of attention to the historical circumstances in the midst of which it was first employed. Christ died, *not*, in the words of the Second Article, 'to reconcile his Father to us;' for He who is Infinite Love and Mercy needed not to be thus reconciled by innocent blood; Christ died, *not* to make an 'atonement' for sin, in the old and still too common heathen sense of this word; *nor* to 'satisfy' the demands of justice or of 'wrath,'†

---

* The reader may compare Archbishop Thomson's defence of the popular theory, in his Essay on the death of Christ in *Aids to Faith*, 4th ed., 1863.

† See Archbishop Thomson's Essay, just referred to.

which otherwise must have fallen upon man, and found their 'satisfaction' in the endless sufferings of the greater portion of our race in the eternal state. So horrible an idea as this is nowhere to be found in the words of any original Christian authority whatever, but only in the curious systems of mediæval theologians and their followers—who certainly, in this case, as in some others, have shown themselves 'wise above what is written.' Christ died, simply that through his death he might enter upon his universal empire, that thus he might 'draw all men' to him, uniting together in one those who before were 'afar off' with them that were already 'nigh,' bringing the 'lost sheep,' not only of 'the house of Israel,' but also of all the outcast nations, into his fold; and thus, again, in a word, 'reconciling' not God to man, but man to God.

It is easy, then, to see why there is no allusion to the supposed 'atoning efficacy' of the cross in the narratives of the crucifixion. It had not entered into the minds of the writers that such a construction of the event was possible. And as to the controversies about the admission of the Gentiles to Christianity, and the legal disqualification under which, to Jewish eyes, they lay, in regard to the promised kingdom, these too were becoming things of the past when the Gospels were written. Hence, doubtless, the silence with which they are passed over; while, at the same time, neither in the actual words of Christ, nor in the narratives of the crucifixion, is there a single expression from which we can justly infer that such a doctrine as that of the atonement, in any modern or orthodox form of it, was in the slightest degree known, or thought of, either by Jesus or by his biographers.

One other fact is deserving of notice. When it is said that Christ died 'for' others, 'the just for the unjust,'* the meaning is, not that he died in their *place*, as their *substitute*, but in their *behalf*, or as their benefactor.† Such is the only meaning which the words convey. And obviously such was the truth. The benefit bestowed was manifest, consisting in the admission to Christianity and consequent reconciliation to God of those who, according to the strong Hebrew prejudices of the time, were 'by nature children of wrath,' 'aliens from the commonwealth of Israel,' unfitted both by their Gentile birth and by actual sins to be received among the disciples of the kingdom. But, by dying and by giving his life, as it were, a 'ransom' for them, Jesus the Christ 'redeemed' them from their out-

* As Rom. v. 6, 7, 8; 1 Pet. iii. 18.

† The preposition used is ὑπερ, and not ἀντι, except in Matt. xx. 28 (parallel with Mark x. 45). Here the idea of *substitution* is by no means clear, though it need not be excluded. The meaning may be the same, as in Matt. xvii. 27, 'Give unto them *for* me and thee' (ἀντὶ ἐμοῦ καὶ σοῦ).

cast state, 'saved' them from their sins, and the punishments awaiting a sinful world. To vary the figure, he 'purchased' them with his blood,* he even 'bore their sins in his own body on the tree.' He was 'made a curse' for them; and by his stripes they were healed. There is a variety of phrases of this kind; none of them surely to be literally accepted, but all to be understood as figures, expressive of the great historical fact which lies at their basis. That fact, once more, is simply this, that Christ died, in order that all men, of every nation, might be admissible, by a new way of justification, that of faith, to his spiritual fold, even though *they* were 'sinners' and Gentiles, and even though *he* were the Hebrew Messiah, born 'under the Law.'

Such then was the 'mystery' of 'Christ crucified,' 'the mystery which had been hid from ages and from generations.'† Its great expounder, the Apostle of the Gentiles, exulted in the light which it was given to him, first and foremost of the apostles, to receive into his mind. He determined to know nothing 'save Jesus Christ and him crucified.'‡ The change of relations thus wrought between God and a sinful world was to him nothing less than a 'new creation;' and, if he wrote the Epistle to the Colossians, he describes in glowing terms the

---

* Acts xx. 28. † 1 Cor i. 23; Col. i. 26.
‡ 1 Cor. ii. 2.

redemption and renewal of all things, through him who was the 'first-born from the dead.'*

But the controversies in which these ideas and this language originated are dead and gone. Except as possessed of historical interest, the modern disciple has little concern with them, and it is, therefore, the greatest possible mistake to construct dogmas and systems of doctrine out of such purely temporary and artificial elements. Still, and evermore, Christianity consists in following him who 'hath words of eternal life;' in earnest and faithful *obedience* to the word and the spirit of Christ. This, indeed, may be learnt, and very clearly, from Paul himself. So the reader will find who will refer to those sections of his Epistles in which he sets forth the duties and the virtues of the Christian life: in which too he shows us, as plainly as words can speak, exactly what Christ himself had taught, namely, that practical love to God and our neighbour is better than all burnt-offerings and sacrifices.†

It is not to be overlooked that the common expression, 'for Christ's sake,' is altogether without example in the New Testament. GOD is never represented there as doing anything whatever 'for Christ's sake,' as, on the popular theory, He ought

* Col. i. 12, *seq.*
† See, in particular, Rom. xii.-xiv.; 1 Cor. xiii.; Gal. v.; Ephes. iv., vi ; Col. iii.

everywhere to have been. The one instance * in which the expression is found, is an acknowledged mistranslation; the words really being, 'even as God *in Christ* hath forgiven you.'

In the foregoing exposition, no attempt has been made to include the peculiar conception of the death of Christ presented by the Epistle to the Hebrews. The statements of that Epistle must, in fact, be regarded simply as the individual and private theory of its unknown author, who does not appear to have contemplated the Gentiles in what he says, and never mentions the great controversy about their admission to Christianity. What he says was applicable only to the Hebrews to whom he wrote, and was no doubt felt by many of them to be highly forcible and appropriate. To us his argument speaks very indirectly. His characteristic expressions are found nowhere else in the New Testament; and being addressed so exclusively to Hebrew readers familiar with the Levitical system, they could not, and did not, become a commanding element in the later development of Christianity, as did the ideas of Paul, and those of the fourth Evangelist. Hence they may safely be left out of the account, in endeavouring to estimate the practical and permanent value of Christianity for our own and for future times.

It would seem to be clear, however, that the writer

* Ephes. iv. 32.

to the Hebrews held the belief in the expiation of sin by the death of Jesus Christ. This was to be expected from one writing so expressly for Jews, and himself educated under the influence of the sacrificial ideas of the ancient Judaism. It is to be noted also that he expresses himself in a very peculiar way throughout the Epistle. Jesus is both the victim offered upon the altar, and also the priest by whom it is offered—not literally so, it is plain, but only in a kind of allegory. Moreover, let it be carefully observed, the sins for which Jesus by his own blood makes atonement, are *past* sins. These are now remitted to those who, by faith, have become his disciples, and they need not hereafter trouble themselves about their former ceremonial observances. If, however, these Hebrew Christians should sin again, after they have 'received the knowledge of the truth,' in that case, they are told, there 're-maineth no more sacrifice for sins.'[*] The sacrifice offered, the atonement made, was once for all. It was not to be from time to time renewed, according to this apostolical writer, even by a 'sacrificing priest,' whether in Greek, or Roman, or Anglican ' orders.'

All this, again, shows us how peculiar and individual is the doctrine of the author of this Epistle ; as also, how radically different, on important points,

[*] Heb. x. 12-27.

are his conceptions from those which find favour with some of our modern controversialists. On these differences, however, it is unnecessary to dwell further in this connection.*

* It has been observed (*supra*, p. 72), that there is no mention of the Gentile controversy in the later writings of the New Testament, except in the form of occasional allusions to the death of Christ, under images derived from the Levitical sacrifices. Such allusions occur in the Epistles which bear the name of Peter, and in the writings attributed to John. It may be, however, that in both of these authors, especially the latter, a true sacrificial efficacy is meant to be ascribed to the death of Christ. The conception of so unique a person as the incarnate Word in John, and of Jesus as the long-expected Messiah in Peter, might well, in those days, be accompanied by the idea of his death having, in some real sense, been an offering by which the sins of mankind were expiated, the Almighty propitiated, and a way opened for the outcast heathen races into his kingdom. This is at least a possible construction of the language now referred to. But yet there is no express statement to this effect in John or Peter, any more than elsewhere; and it is easy to see that the highest Christian idea of God as the all-merciful and loving Father is wholly inconsistent with the old pagan and Jewish notion of propitiation or expiation by means of a sacrifice. Such conceptions, therefore, on this subject, even if held by the writers just named, can only be regarded as transient forms of thought, like the belief in demoniacal possessions. Especially must this be said, if they are seen to be out of harmony with the permanent dictates of reason and religious reverence. Compare, however, John i. 29, 36; 1 John i. 7, ii. 2; 1 Peter i. 18, 19; also several expressions in the book of Revelation, *passim*.

CHAPTER VII.

THE FOURTH GOSPEL—THE WORD MADE FLESH.

In this portion of the New Testament a very different conception of the person and ministry of Jesus is presented to us from that which appears in the three synoptics. It is not requisite, or practicable, to enter minutely into the subject in this place, but a few of the leading considerations are desirable, for the sake of completing the outline here intended to be given.*

In the three synoptics, Jesus appears as a human being endowed with divine powers. He is enabled both to teach the people around him with great effect, and also to perform for them many 'mighty works,' these being usually of a benevolent character, and such as led his disciples and others to recognize him as the expected Messiah. The people also regard him as a 'prophet;' they follow him in crowds, and listen gladly to the words which he speaks to them, in precepts, parables, exhortations, and longer discourses, suitable to the persons and the circumstances around him.

The fourth Gospel gives us little of this peculiar

* For a more complete discussion of this question, the reader is referred to chapters xiv.–xvii. of the work mentioned in the Preface.

portraiture, what resemblance it has to the synoptical account being in general features only, not in details. Jesus works some miracles, it is true; but, with one or two exceptions,* they are different from those of the other Gospels. He delivers no parables such as we have in these—not one. The Baptism is not mentioned, nor the Temptation, nor the Transfiguration.† The teachings of Christ are given partly in the form of controversial discussions with the unbelieving Jews, and also in dialogues and expositions of a very peculiar character with his own disciples. His object usually is to vindicate his own position or authority as the Messiah, and to exhibit, though often in obscure language, his own intimate relations with God—an object of which there is scarcely a trace in the synoptics. The Lord's Prayer is not found in this Gospel, nor anything like it. It is hardly conceivable that the same mind should have expressed itself in the simple and natural language of *that* prayer, and in the form of the prayer attributed to Jesus in chapter xvii. of this Gospel. In John there is no Sermon on the Mount, nor anything approaching it in character; the institution of the Lord's Supper is not mentioned, for it is impossible, in my own judgment, to think that the meal

---

* John vi. 5-13, 19, 20.

† Although John was one of the three apostles present on the occasion. Matt. xvii. 1, *seq.*, and parallels.

described in chapter xiii. is the same with the Passover meal of the synoptics. The memorable scene in Gethsemane is not alluded to; and, in short, there is scarcely any resemblance whatever between the words or even the ideas of Christ which this Evangelist reports, and his various teachings as given by the Three. On the other hand, the Epistles of John are written and conceived exactly in the style of the words attributed to Jesus in the Gospel, and the tone of thought pervading the first Epistle more especially is evidently the very same which occurs in the former, in the various discourses which are found there.

These remarkable phenomena render it impossible to construct a true and natural harmony between the synoptics and the fourth Gospel, as the reader will probably see for himself if he will make the attempt to do so, or if he will examine any of the works in which this attempt has been made. They suggest also the conclusion that this Evangelist has not even intended to compose a strictly historical account of the Ministry, but rather a theological treatise in a narrative form, his great object being simply to set forth and recommend the belief that Jesus was the Christ. This is done in the author's own manner, by the selection of suitable events, and the introduction of such sayings and discourses as might best conduce, in his own judgment, to the end he had in view.

According to this account of the subject before us, the Gospel is not properly a historical work at all, in any strict sense of this expression, although it most probably contains some historical materials. It is rather a theological argument, in the form of a history; and its great purpose is what is stated at the close of chapter xx. in the words, 'These are written, that ye might believe that Jesus is the Christ, the Son of God, and that believing ye might have life through his name.' It may be added, that the discourses and the prayer of Jesus in this Gospel are in all probability the composition of the Evangelist. It is well known to have been the custom, with historical and other writers of his age, to ascribe to those of whom they wrote conversations and speeches such as were considered suitable to their characters and circumstances.*

However this may be, the differences between the first three Gospels and the fourth are such as to make it necessary to consider the latter as a sub-

---

* Compare, in illustration, the so-called *Recognitions of Clement*, which were written about a century later than the Gospel, and which have been recently characterized in the following terms: 'The writer of the work seems to have had no intention of presenting his statements as facts; but choosing the disciples of Christ and their followers as his principal characters, he has put into their mouths the most important of his beliefs, and woven the whole together by a fictitious narrative." — *Ante-Nicene Library*, Introductory Notice to the *Recognitions*.

stantive work, by itself; and to read and interpret many of its words and phrases, not in the light of the other Gospels, but in that of certain well-known philosophical conceptions and speculations with which its author was unquestionably familiar.

This is more particularly seen in the introduction to the Gospel. Here it is shown that in Jesus the Divine Word (Logos) 'became flesh and dwelt among us.' The conception of the Word was a familiar one in the ancient world at the time when the Gospel was written, and long before. It is not in its origin a Christian conception; let this be especially observed by the reader. It is a product of Gentile or heathen speculation. In illustration of this statement, it will be sufficient to cite the following words from an eminent authority. Dr. Burton, in his Bampton Lectures, speaking of certain emanations from the Divine Mind called Æons, writes as follows: 'One of these Æons was termed Logos; and we may say with truth that between the genuine followers of Plato and the corruptors of his doctrine, the Gnostics, the whole learned world, at the time of our Saviour's death, from Athens to Alexandria, and from Rome to Asia Minor, was beset with philosophical systems, in every one of which the term Logos held a conspicuous place.' *

* *Bampton Lectures* (by Dr. E. Burton, Regius Professor at Oxford), 1829, p. 215.

What was meant exactly by the Word, or Logos, in the time of St. John, it is difficult to state to the reader in few words. It may be learnt in various ancient authors; and especially in the pages of the Jewish Philo of Alexandria, who lived in the first century of the Christian era, and was for a part of his life a contemporary of Christ and the apostles. This writer has anticipated the Evangelist in saying, respecting the Divine Word, all that is said in the proem of the Gospel, and a good deal besides. A Bampton Lecturer of our own day gives the following account: '.... the term Logos denotes at the very least something intimately and everlastingly present with God, something as internal to the being of God as thought is to the soul of man. In truth, the Divine Logos is God reflected in his own eternal Thought; in the Logos, God is his own Object. This Infinite Thought, the reflection and counterpart of God, subsisting in God as a Being or Hypostasis, and having a tendency to self-communication—such is the Logos. The Logos is the Thought of God, not intermittent and precarious like human thought, but subsisting with the intensity of a personal form.'* It does not appear what this learned writer means exactly by saying that the Word 'subsisted in God as a Being or Hypostasis, having a

* Liddon, *Bampton Lectures*, pp. 228, 229 (smaller edition, 1868).

tendency to self-communication,' and 'with the intensity of a personal form.' Nor does he tell us where precisely he obtained this subtle piece of divine philosophy; but he is, no doubt, very near the truth when he writes that the Word was, or was conceived of as, 'the Thought of God;' and also when he says, in the same passage, that the Word was not 'an independent being existing externally to the One God,' adding that so to conceive of it 'would be an error at issue with the first truth of monotheism.' It cannot be doubted that this is a just representation. But then does it not provoke the suggestion that it would be well, therefore, not to *speak* of the Word as 'an independent being,' possessed of a separate personal existence; not even to conceive of it under this polytheistic character, and much less to address it continually in *prayers* and hymns, exactly as if it *were* 'an independent being, existing externally to the One God?'

The truth, then, would appear to be, that the Word or Logos was the form under which the thought or reason or mind of God was conceived of, especially as it manifested itself outwardly in creation and providence. According to the fundamental tenets of the philosophy in which this mode of conception originated, the Supreme God could not come into contact, or into any close relations, with gross and sinful matter, in creation or otherwise. To avoid the supposition of this, it was said that his Word came forth from Him and acted for Him. But what was really meant by such expressions was, nevertheless, only that God acted or manifested Himself. Then, in the course of time, this divine, self-revealing faculty, the thought of the Infinite Mind, was hypostatized, that is, conceived of and represented as a *personal* being, and is even spoken of by Philo not only as the 'Son of God,' and the first begotten Son, but also as a 'second God.' But then, again, this writer was a Jew, and it is scarcely probable that he intended really to make *two* Gods; though, indeed, we can perhaps hardly judge what might seem probable or possible in those days of unbridled speculation. He may, therefore, have conceived of the Word, in its character of a separate personal being, only in a kind of improper or figurative sense; and he goes back, from time to time, to speak of it still as only a *power*, or manifestation, of the One Supreme. In reference to this question, Dr. Liddon observes that a study of certain passages in Philo will 'convince any unprejudiced reader that Philo did not know his own mind; that his Logos was sometimes impersonal and sometimes not, or that he sometimes *thought* of a personal Logos and never *believed* in one.' * This is a convenient way of settling the point, so far as Philo is concerned.

* *Bampton Lectures*, pp. 66, 67.

The fact, however, remains and cannot be too distinctly kept in view, and cannot be got rid of on any supposition whatever, that the doctrine of the Word was not in its origin a doctrine of Christian revelation, and that we do not owe that doctrine to Christianity at all, but to heathen philosophy. Nevertheless, the fourth Evangelist, for reasons of which he has not informed us, adopted this conception. He did so, we may conjecture, out of regard to the persons for whom he wrote the Gospel. They would be familiar with that way of conceiving of God and His active manifestation of Himself in the world; and so the Evangelist, when he intended to say that divine power from God was with Jesus and in him, expresses this by telling us that the Word was in him, was 'made flesh' in him—the same Word which was in the beginning with God, and was in truth God Himself.*

Such being the fundamental conception of the

---

* It has been a question, and it must be so, whether the Evangelist, in v. 1 of the Gospel, meant to say 'the Word was God,' or only 'the Word was a god,' that is, a divine being. Important considerations, which can scarcely be introduced here, lead to the latter interpretation of his statement; but, nevertheless, in the above-given exposition the usual orthodox view of his meaning has been accepted as correct—the result being to *identify* GOD and the Word; in other words, to consider as *one*, GOD and the Thought or Reason of his own mind: according to the Evangelist's statement, 'the Word was God.'

Gospel, it was but a little step further to represent Jesus as acting and speaking in harmony with it. Accordingly in Him 'the Word was made flesh, and dwelt among us:' he is the incarnate Logos. The Logos is not only hypostatized and personified, as in the earlier verses of the Gospel, but it is present upon earth in Jesus, as appears from many expressions of this Evangelist. Jesus says, for example, 'I came down from heaven not to do mine own will, but the will of him that sent me:' he says, 'Before Abraham was, I am' (or probably, 'I am *he*,' that is, the pre-ordained Messiah).*
He speaks of the glory which he had with God 'before the world was;' and Thomas, addressing him after the resurrection, is represented as saying, 'My Lord and my God.'†

It is to be noted, however, that while the Evangelist thus represents Jesus as the Word 'made flesh,' he does not refrain from saying that the Father Himself was present in him. The words

---

* John viii. 58; compare John viii. 24, 28, with iv. 26, ix. 9; also Mark xiii. 6, xiv. 62. There is no reference in viii. 58, to Exod. iii. 14, as often supposed. See Appendix, Note F.

† John vi. 38, viii. 58, xvii. 5, xx. 28; compare viii. 42, xiii. 3, xvi. 27. John iii. 13 may be a parenthesis by the Evangelist. Compare the introduction of the Epistle to the Hebrews, in which is found the same conception of the personality of the divine Son who, in the next chapter of the Epistle, is identified with Jesus.

that he speaks he has heard from the Father; his works are not his own, but the Father's that sent Him. He says, too, 'I and my Father are one.' From such expressions it appears that the Word in Jesus was conceived of as equivalent to the presence of the Father, of God Himself, in him; insomuch that Jesus can even say, 'He that hath seen Me hath seen the Father.' The two forms of expression are probably identical in force, being each of them intended simply to convey the one idea of the divine power in Jesus; to state that it was *this* which made him what he was. At one time, it is the Father that acts through him; at another it is the Word; but the two statements are really, in value, one and the same.

It thus appears that the interpretation of this Gospel is not so difficult as it might at first sight appear, when it is remembered that the Evangelist has borrowed from the Gentile philosophy a peculiar mode of speaking of the divine presence and action, and has applied it to the person of Christ. In so doing, it may be added, he cannot have intended to lead his readers to think that Jesus was personally God, but only that he was the chosen instrument of the divine wisdom and goodness to the world; that, in other words, God was with him, enabling him to speak as 'never man spake,' and to do the works which no man could do, unless God were with him.*

Some, however, while substantially adopting this mode of explanation, have yet, in one respect, gone a little farther. It has been held that the Evangelist did intend to distinguish between God and the Word, so far as actually to make a separate and subordinate personal being of the latter, the first and greatest of all created existences, and to represent this as incarnate upon the earth in Jesus. This view of the subject is closely related to the ancient Arian idea of the person of Christ, and those who hold it as an absolute or permanent truth of religion may very properly call themselves after the great Nicene heresiarch. The serious objection to it as a doctrine of Christianity is, that it is entirely absent from the first three Gospels, as it is also from the authentic writings of St. Paul.† This could not have been the case had it been the literal truth. Doubtless, therefore, the correct explanation is, that the representation of the fourth Gospel is a peculiar mode of conception only, to which the Evangelist was led by circumstances of which we are not informed. The actual truth of fact which he designed to convey to his readers could, in short, be

---

* Compare John iii. 1, 2.

† It may be the conception of Heb. i., a passage which is clearly in essential harmony with the Logos doctrine.

no other than that which is contained in the synoptical Gospels, and which was expressed by Peter on the day of Pentecost, when he used the words, 'Jesus of Nazareth, a man approved of God among you, by miracles and wonders and signs which God did by him in the midst of you, as ye yourselves also know.'*

It is not to be overlooked, as a final consideration in this connection, that Jesus is represented on two occasions, even in this Gospel, as calling the Almighty Father the 'only' God. The first of these is a little kept out of sight in the English version, which runs thus:—'How can ye believe, which receive honour one of another, and seek not the honour that cometh from God only?' The latter words should be, 'that cometh from the only God.' The other instance is near the beginning of the prayer in chapter xvii. :—'Father, the hour is come; .... and this is life eternal that they might know thee, the only true God, and Jesus Christ whom Thou hast sent.'†

The bearing of the foregoing statements upon the Nicene Creed will not escape the reader's notice. They tend directly to establish the fact that the characteristic doctrine of that Creed—which speaks of Jesus Christ as 'God of God, light of light, very God of very God'—is largely, in its origin and

---

* Acts ii. 22.   † John v. 44, xvii. 1-3.

essence, a product of heathen philosophy. It is well known, indeed, that the Creed itself was drawn up, or rather sanctioned, by a Council presided over by an unbaptized Emperor—by one, too, who was baptized at last by an Arian bishop.*

CHAPTER VIII.

BAPTISM—BAPTISMAL REGENERATION.

Conspicuous among the words of Jesus Christ, are those which are found near the close of the first Gospel, and which are often termed the Baptismal Formula. In our English version they are as follows: 'Go ye, therefore, and teach all nations, baptizing them in the name of the Father, and of the Son, and of the Holy Ghost.' More exactly rendered, the word 'into' will be read for 'in;' as many also will prefer the expression 'Holy Spirit' to 'Holy Ghost,' as a more intelligible and adequate representation of the original word.*

* See Dean Stanley's *Eastern Church*, Lect. vi.; comp. Hefele, *History of Councils*, book ii.

† The poor and almost obsolete word 'Ghost' is only allowable from long-descended habit and association. So far as its retention is designed to convey the idea of *personality* more distinctly than is done by 'Spirit,' it is altogether unjustifiable, as being unfaithful to the Scripture. The original is everywhere the *same* Greek word πνεῦμα; and probably the

Baptism was an ancient rite of the Jews. It had been long in use before it was adopted as a solemn and formal mode of admitting disciples to the profession of Christianity. From various scriptural expressions we know that baptism into a person or object was equivalent to the reception of the disciple into the religion with which that person or object was, in some way, associated or identified. The Jews of old are designated by St. Paul as having been 'baptized into Moses.' The same apostle speaks of the Christians of his day as those who 'were baptized into' the death of Christ. John the Baptist received the people who came to him, to his own baptism 'into repentance;' and there were disciples of his, long after Christ's death, who had been baptized only 'into John's baptism.'*

Baptism, then, into a person or object included the recognition, or confession, of either, in whatever religious character properly belonged to them. Hence 'into the name of Jesus,'† it implied the confession of him as the Christ; in other words, the confession of him as 'the Son of God,'—a well-understood appellation of the Messiah. Thus, too,

English Authorized Version stands alone among versions in giving a twofold rendering (sometimes 'Ghost,' sometimes 'Spirit') to so important an expression. Comp. Rom. viii. 1, *seq.*; 1 Cor. xii. 3.

* 1 Cor. x. 2; Rom. vi. 3; Matt. iii. 6–11; Acts xix. 3.
† Acts viii. 16, xix. 5.

the injunction to baptize 'into the name of the Father' signified and included the acknowledgment of the Almighty Father as revealed by Christ; the acknowledgment of Him as the One God and Father of all men alike, without respect of persons. The acknowledgment of the Holy Spirit, too, was of especial importance in the early days of Christianity. By many it had been denied that our Lord did his 'mighty works' by divine power,* and they referred them to evil spirits. In later times, the Spirit is said to have been *given* to the disciples. Hence, again, the convert was baptized 'into the Holy Spirit.' He was thus taught to recognize a twofold fact; first, that it was the Spirit of God Himself in Jesus, and not any evil spirit, that was with him throughout his life; and secondly, that the same divine help and power was, in still later times, given to his disciples. Such, in few words, appear to have been the ideas under which the threefold form of baptism originated; the ideas which, so far as can be gathered from the sacred history itself, this form was intended to embody and convey.

In our own time, it will, to most readers, be evident, we can employ the expression only in a kind of secondary sense. We may baptize into the name of the Heavenly Father; of the Son by whom He has been best revealed to us; and of that Holy

* Luke xi. 15, *seq.*

Spirit of God by which, acting in our hearts to help and guide and comfort, our highest ideas and principles of right and duty are given to us, and made sure and abiding influences in our lives. In such a use of the phrase we approximate to the primitive Christian meaning of the words. But it is not exactly the *same* use of them; and cannot be, because no one, in these times, partakes of those outward manifestations of the Spirit of which the New Testament history so often speaks.

It is, however, worthy of special remark, that in no single instance in the New Testament do we read of the so-called 'baptismal formula' having been employed. The baptism of converts is in several instances mentioned in the book of Acts; but it is always 'into the name of Jesus,' or also 'in the name of Jesus,'[*]—almost as if the longer form of words had not yet come into use, or else had fallen into disuse. In either case, we may infer that it had never been known or regarded in those early times as an express form, authoritatively enjoined and always to be employed,—according to the notion which prevails in some quarters at the present day.

It seems clear, then, that it is altogether wrong to consider these words as a fixed formula never to be departed from. Evidently such was not the understanding of the early Christians. If such a use had

[*] Acts viii. 16, x. 47, 48, xix. 5.

been intended by the founder of Christianity, without doubt this would have been plainly expressed, and the needful record of the intention would surely have been preserved for us in the books of the New Testament.

But, passing on from this consideration, it may next be noticed that since the apostolic age the rite of Baptism has very materially changed its character. In the first instance, it was administered only to adults, not to infants or young children. There is no instance in the New Testament of its administration to any one who was not able, at least as regarded his years, intelligently to acknowledge Jesus of Nazareth as the Christ. Baptism into *his* name meant *that*, simply, and could not therefore be properly given to a child.

Another respect in which the rite is greatly changed is in regard to what it signifies, or what is confessed by those who receive it. With young children, indeed, it has no signification at all in which they can participate, or which they can acknowledge. They simply know nothing about it. But, even for adults who receive it, its import has somewhat changed. It is not now the confession of Jesus the Christ, the Son of God, in the old historical sense, that is intended; for the inquiry whether he was so or not, or in what sense he was so, probably never occurs to even an up-grown person baptized in our day, any more than to those who perform the ceremony. All this is taken for granted; while the service is looked upon simply as a formal and outward profession of what is understood to be the Christian religion,—more especially of those great doctrines which are usually supposed, in our time, to constitute the essentials of Christian faith.

But the confession, in baptism, of an elaborate system of orthodox dogmas, I need not say, nowhere makes its appearance in the New Testament. This negative position, however, is one of which detailed proof cannot here be given. It is only to be verified by reading the early history of Christianity, as presented in the sacred books. But there it will be seen, so far as anything clearly appears at all, that the one especial profession made or implied in baptism was that of belief in Jesus of Nazareth as the expected Christ.*

This very considerable difference in the substance of the baptismal confession is not, however, the only change which has passed over this ancient service. In the Churches of Rome and of England, in particular, it has assumed a complexion of a very remarkable kind, and one of which there is no trace whatever in the New Testament. I suppose every

---

* See the probably spurious but ancient verse, Acts viii. 37; compare ii. 22–41, ix. 20, 22, xvi. 31, 33.

one is familiar with the doctrine of baptism set forth more especially by our own Established Church. The Catechism and the Baptismal Service alike reveal to us what it is.

The child is born in sin—subject to that depravation of nature wrought in the human race by the transgression of the first parents. It is, therefore, by birth, a child, not of God, but of Satan; naturally a member, not of the kingdom of heaven, but only of that infernal kingdom reserved for the devil and his angels. Thus, to speak quite plainly, the new-born infant is under the wrath of God; and liable—I will not say to what it is liable, for ever and ever. Such is the theory;—the doctrine, more or less strongly expressed, or taken for granted, in the two authoritative formularies above referred to. Whether any one *believes* it, is another question altogether, and one which I scarcely like to touch; or whether it is only kept up and professed or conformed to, as a relic of antique faith which cannot easily be got rid of. This latter may be its true character; and if so, those who, by official position and the words they have to use, would seem to be bound to profess such a doctrine, are certainly deserving of commiseration;—so utterly wanting as it is in truth and religious reverence; so entirely contrary to Christian ideas of right and wrong; so dishonouring alike to God and man!

But, dreadful as the theory is of the natural state of the infant, let not any one be greatly disturbed on account of it. It is only a kind of grotesque though horrible fiction, after all; not distantly akin to the once popular beliefs in witchcraft and demoniacal possession. And I should suppose that, with the growth of knowledge, people who think seriously upon the subject, and are not afraid to use the eyes of their reason, must increasingly see the matter in this light.

At any rate, in case there be real believers in this old-fashioned doctrine, there is little occasion for any of them to be much distressed by his belief. Alarming as the condition of the new-born infant may be, there is a cheap and easy way of releasing him from it. This, according to the same ingenious theory, is by the way of baptism. The same theory, as it appears in the Catechism and the Baptismal Service, shows us that the priest has power, by this rite, at once to transform the young child of Satan into a child of God. For this end, it is only necessary to have recourse to the sprinkling of a little water by the hand of a rightly ordained official; and, lo! forthwith the child is 'regenerate and grafted into the body of Christ;' its native depravity is mystically washed away; it is delivered from God's 'wrath,' made a 'member of Christ, the child of God, and an inheritor of the kingdom of heaven.' These expressions are repeated from the established forms, and so there need be no doubt as to the effect intended to be produced. But whether any one, except, perhaps, the most uninformed and unreflecting, believes in it or not, is quite a different matter. If it is not believed, certainly it ought not to be professed by any one; only, it is to be remembered, there are Acts of Parliament in the way of laying it aside, and other serious obstacles. These are very potent, if not to produce belief, at least to encourage profession;* and so we may, alas! anticipate, many will go on professing and professing, and perhaps trying to believe even against belief, until some day, at length, there comes an earthquake, or some great revulsion of feeling equivalent to an earthquake, and suddenly

* It may be thought that the Gorham Judgment legally releases all official persons, who choose to be so released, from the necessity of believing the words they employ in the Baptismal Service,—from believing them, or professing to believe them, in their natural sense. Granting this, how does that Judgment affect the parents? Do not *they*, in multitudes of cases, understand the words in their natural sense, and believe them too? Most of them have probably never heard of the Gorham Judgment; and hence the sad spectacle, daily presented to the nation, of officiating ministers of religion using the words of a solemn Service in one sense, while others engaged in the same Service understand them in another. That this is so, is shown by the common superstition which renders many parents so anxious to have a child baptized as soon as practicable after birth, to prevent the possibility of its dying unbaptized, *i.e.* unregenerate.

puts an end to it all. And surely, it may be added, the sooner this arrives, the better for the interests of truth and sincerity of thought and speech. Even Acts of Parliament ought not to be allowed to stand in the way of these; and those who do not believe ought certainly to let their unbelief be made known from time to time—loudly and distinctly known, in order that the needed change may be brought about by the ecclesiastical or other authorities who have the power to make it.

Until this day comes, those whose lot it is merely to look on, as it were, at these things from a distance have at least the comfort of thinking that the simple and beautiful rite of baptism is not by any necessity associated with a superstition which is discreditable to an enlightened age. We may retain the good and true without necessarily adopting the error and the evil; for, in this case as in many more, there is a just mean between unbelief and rejection on the one hand, and ignorant credulity or blind fetichism on the other.

In our established system there is another singular usage which it may be allowed to me to mention in this connection; more especially as it is the parent of much that is delusive, and tends by its character to drive many persons away from the baptismal ceremony altogether. The usual Church Service for the baptism of infants contains at least an implied acknowledgment that the rite signifies, or ought to signify, the confession by the baptized person of Jesus Christ, or, again, the acceptance by the former of the religion of Jesus Christ. But how can such an acknowledgment be made by a young child—an infant, perhaps, of a few days old? To meet this, our national system makes the provision of godfathers and godmothers. It is difficult to characterize this institution. From one point of view, it is a sensible and a beautiful arrangement; from another, it is worse than useless, and even injurious to the sincerity and truthfulness of all concerned.

The godfathers and godmothers undertake to say and do for the infant what it cannot say or do for itself. In later years, the Catechism makes the child declare of its sponsors, 'They did promise and vow three things in my name: First, that I should renounce the devil and all his works, the pomps and vanities of this wicked world, and all the sinful lusts of the flesh; secondly, that I should believe all the articles of the Christian faith; and thirdly, that I should keep God's holy will and commandments, and walk in the same all the days of my life.' Excellent promises, if they were only performed! But *are* they performed? Do godfathers and godmothers, as the rule, see that the child is taught and trained in all that they have undertaken to look to?

I need not answer this question; for it is matter of common remark and experience, how little the engagements which have been solemnly taken are ever thought of again by multitudes; how lightly they are entered into; and, in short, what a mere empty form these engagements of the Baptismal Service have become to most of the persons who enter into them.

Such, however, are the facts; and the whole affords a mournful illustration of the utter hollowness of much in our national system of Christianity, —a system which so obviously comes down to us from times of much faith and little reflection, and which, in some respects, is so greatly out of harmony with the ideas and usages of modern life.

There is a minor point which, in the presence of these graver considerations, is not worth many words. It is the difference between ancient and modern baptizing, as regards the manner in which the rite is administered; whether by immersion, or by sprinkling simply. There can be no doubt as to what was the ancient Jewish custom; but then this custom was suited to the warm climate of Palestine and the East, and is not suited to the cold climate of many parts of Europe, including our own country. The difference would scarcely be worth notice, were it not that some persons have been, and perhaps are, in the habit of refusing to admit to the Lord's Supper any but those who have been baptized in the ancient Judaic way. It is doubtless for every one to judge for himself, and to do what is right in his own eyes, —for himself, though not for another. If, however, he be led to think that another is not as good a Christian as himself, because he does not accept the same ideas of baptism, then he must not be surprised if he finds himself exposed to the rebuke which is due to bigotry, and which they very richly deserve who exalt the letter above the spirit, or mere form and ceremony above the substance of that obedience which is better than sacrifice.*

It remains to say a few words as to the true nature of this ancient rite, regarded as one which

---

* These remarks, I need scarcely observe, are applicable in the strongest degree to those lamentable instances of intolerance which occasionally offend the public sense of decency— in the refusal, on the part of a certain section of the national clergy, to read the Burial Service over one who has not been baptized according to the forms of the Church of England. Those who thus offend are mostly the same persons who claim to be emphatically the successors of the Apostles. Yet, on their avowed principles, they would refuse to acknowledge the sufficiency of baptism administered according to the form which alone is met with in the Acts of the Apostles. Here, as before pointed out, the threefold formula never occurs, but that only ' in (or into) the name of Jesus Christ.'

[The correctness of the first sentence of this note has been denied by a reviewer in the *John Bull* newspaper of July 8, 1874. Many examples, however, of the refusal alluded to may be produced: see the Pamphlet of Mr. J. Carvell Williams, *A plea for a Free Churchyard* (1870), pp. 18-22.]

can still be retained among Christian people with reasonable purpose and propriety. It is, in truth, a service of dedication; an expression of the desire of Christian parents to train up their children in the fear of God, and as disciples of Jesus Christ. It is a solemnly expressed desire to this effect; and it may be of the utmost utility as a serious and deliberate expression of that desire. But it is gross superstition to suppose that baptism can make any difference to the innocent child, who, we may well believe, is as much a child of God before the ceremony as after. It is right also to remember that we cannot always effectually transfer into our modern life and our modern ways of thinking, either the ideas or the religious usages of the Jews of Palestine, in the first century of the Christian era. In many a case, all that can be done is to endeavour to follow and imitate the devout and earnest spirit which they so often manifest, and which frequently led them to sacrifice everything that was most dear to them for the sake of what they believed to be the cause of God and of His truth. Outward forms must be allowed to change from generation to generation, and may best be left free to do so. Happy will it be for our times, and the people of our times, if they will duly remember this; and, while seeking to adopt such forms of expression and outward ritual as altered feelings and circumstances require, if, along with these, they will strive to cherish still the ancient feelings of charity and piety embodied even in rites or institutions which, as time goes on, it may become necessary to alter and modify, or altogether to lay aside, and replace by something else.

CHAPTER IX.

PERMANENT ELEMENT IN THE LIFE AND WORDS OF CHRIST.

THE belief that Jesus of Nazareth was the expected Christ, formed the doctrinal *nucleus* of the early Christianity. Such was the primitive Christian 'faith,'* the substance of the Gospel, without which a man could not be a Christian, and, as a consequence, could not be 'saved,' at the anticipated second coming of the Messiah to judge the world.† From the same belief evidently arose the name 'Christian;' those who received Jesus as Christ being fitly called CHRIST-ians.

---

* This word is also employed in the New Testament in a wider sense, as faith in God, faith in Jesus as his messenger. Thus Heb. xi. 1, *seq.*; John xvi. 30, 31; Rom. iv. 3, 16. But wherever a specific Christian faith is meant, it is what is stated above.

† Compare Matt. xxv. 31, *seq.*; Mark xvi. 15, 16; Luke xii. 35–40; Acts iii. 19–21; 1 Cor. xv. 51, *seq.*; 1 Thess. iv. 13, v. 10.

In the fourth Gospel, the open assumption of the Messianic character is attributed to Jesus himself, in several instances, and from the beginning.* The woman of Samaria, for example, observes, 'When Messias cometh which is called Christ . . . he will tell us all things;' Jesus replies, 'I that speak unto thee am *he*.' He says to Mary, 'Whosoever liveth and believeth in me, shall never die. Believest thou this?' She answers, 'Yea, Lord, I believe that thou art the Christ, the Son of God, which should come into the world.'† To the Jews he says, 'If ye believe not that I am *he*, ye shall die in your sins.'‡ In these and other instances, in the fourth Gospel, the speaker clearly avows his Messiahship. In the synoptics, however, he would appear rather to have refrained from doing so; at least he sometimes enjoins his disciples not to make known to others the fact that he was Christ.§ Shortly before his last Passover, and also at his trial, he assumes this title in the most public manner, and allows

* John i. 49, 50; comp. v. 34.
† John xi. 26, 27.
‡ John viii. 24; comp. v. 28; also v. 58, meaning 'I am *he*.' See also Acts ix. 20–22, xviii. 28; also Appendix, Note F.
§ Matt. xvi. 20, and parallels; comp. Matt. xii. 16, and similar places. It is not, however, to be overlooked that the use of the expression, 'Son of Man,' would no doubt suggest the assumption of the Messianic character.

the people to salute him as the 'Son of David.' In what sense he most probably did so, has been noticed above, in Chapter V.

With this early confession of Jesus as the Christ, the 'Son of God,' or also, 'Son of Man' (for these, too, were usual appellations of the same personage),* were united some other ideas which, though of great power in the first instance, were not destined to a permanent existence. Some of these have been already noticed. They were, for example, the continued authority of the Law,— over Gentile converts in particular; the temporal character of the Messiah's kingdom; the speedy return of the departed Saviour to judge the world, to reign personally in the midst of his chosen people, and also to execute vengeance upon their enemies and oppressors. These latter anticipations were, without question, essential elements of the faith of the early disciples,† and formed a lever in their hands to move the world. But yet these beliefs, like the others, were in time to lose their power and pass away from view. The prejudice, again, that none but Jews, or converts to Judaism, should become disciples, was for some time possessed of the utmost vitality. It was, nevertheless, to be laid aside, and it is now a thing

---

* Appendix, Note E.
† See the book of Revelation, chapters xviii.–xx.

of the past—too much, indeed, left out of sight by modern interpreters of the Christian books.

But what then remains to us from the primitive Christianity? A great statesman of our day has recently laid his hand upon what he evidently thinks entitled to be considered the most certain and durable element of the Christian religion; for he tells us that 'more than ninety-nine in every hundred Christians have with one voice confessed the Deity and Incarnation of our Lord as the cardinal and central truths of our Religion.'*

* *Address* at the Liverpool College, by the Right Hon. W. E. Gladstone, M.P. (1872), p. 28.—Mr. Gladstone's words are these: '. . . . If the divisions among Christians are remarkable, not less so is their unity in the greatest doctrines that they hold. Well nigh fifteen hundred years . . . . have passed away, since the great controversies concerning the Deity and the Person of the Redeemer were, after a long agony, determined. As before that time in a manner less defined, but adequate for their day, so ever since that time, amid all the chance and change, more, aye more, than ninety-nine in every hundred Christians have with one voice confessed the Deity and Incarnation of our Lord as the cardinal and central truths of our Religion.'

With all due respect to so eminent a name, this, I must say, appears to me to be a hasty and ill-considered statement—unless, indeed, Mr. Gladstone intended to limit the 'Christians' of whom he speaks to a comparatively select body, defined by himself, out of all the countless millions of nominal professors of Christianity throughout the world. Granting, however, for a moment, the numerical correctness of his statement, how shall it be considered conclusive, as Mr. Gladstone implies that it is, in regard to the *truth* of the doctrines which

But then it is capable of historical demonstration, and it has been sufficiently shown in the preceding chapter, that these alleged 'truths' are

he mentions? He, doubtless, does not need to be reminded that *numbers* are no sure test of truth. Or, if he thinks that they are, would he like to estimate and to tell us, what proportion of the 'ninety-nine in every hundred' receive *along with* those doctrines, that of Transubstantiation, the worship of the 'Mother of God,' and the infallibility of the Pope? And shall we accept these latter doctrines, too, on the same overwhelming authority?

But, in truth, the assertion now in question is one which will not bear any close examination. For, take sceptical Germany, take unbelieving France, take Italy, Spain, Holland, and other countries that might be named, and will any one venture to affirm, of the *more thoughtful and instructed* people in these different lands, that ninety-nine out of every hundred of them confess the doctrines referred to? And even among the devouter millions of Christians, whether in Roman Catholic or in Protestant countries—including all the women and children, ignorant and instructed alike—is not the confession spoken of much on a par with the general acceptance of certain well-known scientific doctrines,—that, for example, of gravitation, or that of the Copernican system of the universe? It is, therefore, of absolutely no value whatever as an attestation by thoughtful, well-informed minds. These persons believe simply because they have been brought up to believe; they accept, not with any intelligent, well-grounded conviction, but because their belief has been impressed upon them from without, like the impression of a seal upon the unresisting wax, by the inculcation or the mere imitation of others. What then is it worth as evidence of the truth of either of the great doctrines named by Mr. Gladstone, in the orthodox sense of those expressions?

There is another most serious consideration. Among the most eminent scientific men of our time, in all countries, are not in fact a part of the primitive Christianity at all, but a mere growth, a slow and long-contested growth, of human speculation, under the immediate suggestion and fostering influence of Gentile philosophy. Mr. Gladstone himself speaks of that growth as a 'long agony;' and such, in truth, it was;—a long agony, in which the defeated party were neither more nor less than the representatives, from time to time, of the older and more genuine ideas and facts of the primitive Gospel. The words of Christ, as reported in the three oldest records of his life, contain no trace of these doctrines, but very much that is quite inconsistent with them; and the same is true, differently expressed, of the fourth Gospel also. How then shall it be held that even these so-called 'cardinal and central truths,' widely accepted as no doubt they are, shall stand for ever as the absolute truth?

But is there then *nothing* left to us of this firm and durable character? And is the great hope of 'one fold and one shepherd,' only a baseless dream after all? Surely, so desponding an answer need not to be given to our question; for the Spirit and the Word of Christ are still left to us—that Spirit without which, as Paul declares, we are 'none of

these doctrines commonly received or commonly rejected?—and in which direction does the tendency now run with thoughtful persons—to their reception or their rejection?

his;' that Word which the Master himself assures us, 'shall not pass away.'

'Before all things,' the SPIRIT OF CHRIST! And what this was, and is, it requires no detailed exposition to set forth. Christian men are everywhere agreed as to its most vital and characteristic qualities. It is the spirit of truth and justice and fidelity to the sense of duty; of love and goodwill between man and man, of humble faith and reliance upon God. It is this, manifested in practical obedience and well-doing, in self-renunciation and sympathy for the afflicted and suffering. It is tender compassion for the sinner, combined with an earnest intolerance of untruth, hypocrisy, and formality, in religion as in everything else. It is the spirit of prayer and upward aspiration towards the Universal Father, of unfailing submission to the Holy Will and devout trust in the unseen heaven; while at last, as the result and crown of all, it is a perfect readiness, even in the moment of supreme agony and death, to commit every interest and care of earthly life into the hands of God,—not forgetting, withal, to return good for evil, blessing and forgiveness for injury and scorn, as shown in that memorable prayer, 'Father, forgive them, they know not what they do.'

Such are the lessons to be learnt from the words and the deeds of the Teacher. And, with these before us, need we any of us be in doubt as to what is the imperishable essence of Christianity? or helplessly say, as some do, that we cannot find it out? or declare that we can only see it where in truth it is hardly to be seen at all,—in creeds and dogmas and Church organizations which breathe the spirit of exclusion and denunciation? Surely not so; but Christianity stands before us in Christ, living, acting, and speaking, in his thoughts, his words, his daily life.

This lofty and divine spirit, embodied, so to speak, in Jesus Christ, and often inspired, as it has been, in others by his transmitted influence, is without question the highest and most precious memorial of his ministry. So much is this the case that the word *Christian* itself has been usually understood to denote the ideal of human excellence—although, also, it is too true that many so-called Christians are unworthy of the term. To express that ideal, we do not employ the name of Plato or of Socrates, or any other name of ancient or modern times, however great and commanding it may be. We simply use the name of Christ. We say *Christian* and *Christ-like;* and I have no doubt whatever, the world will continue to do this, and increasingly do it, the more justly and naturally his words and spirit are appreciated. No one, in short, who reviews even the imperfect record of his career left to us in the Gospels, can doubt the purity, elevation, and devoutness of his mind, or his self-sacrificing zeal and love towards God and man; or can hesitate to admit that even such as he was himself he desired that his disciples should be,—as many of them, I must add, *have* been.

This, then, it must be,—not any mere dogma, or any creed* or confession of faith which human pen can write,—this it must be, which is the abiding element of Christ's religion. This, too, we may well believe, it is, which the Almighty wisdom has *intended* to set before the world in him, stamped with divine approval, as the great and practical issue of his ministry. And this position may be held with the greater confidence because it is plain that, if the providential design in Christ were to lead men to think upon his spirit, to admire and reverence, and at least aspire to imitate, such is, in fact, the actual end which has been, and is more and more being, accomplished. So much is this the case, that even in this consists the *one* aspect of Christianity in regard to which all Christian men of every church and sect are *agreed*,—agreed as they certainly are not in anything else.

And, I would briefly ask in passing, Does not this virtual agreement in the greatest thing of all afford a sufficient foundation on which a CHURCH might be

---

* Let the reader, however, compare, if he will, the wonderful assertions of the Athanasian Creed.

built, to be named after Christ?—a Church wide enough to take in all Christian men who are contented to follow Him, and who desire to be filled and guided by his spirit? It is not indeed that, in such a communion, all would think alike, on the various points of theological doctrine. This, for the present, is not possible, nor is it necessary, or even to be desired. But yet, as Christian disciples, might we not—even a whole nation—stand together, in our worshipping assemblies, upon the common principle of allegiance to the one spiritual Lord, combined, nevertheless, with 'the liberty wherewith Christ has made us free?' Might not each separate congregation, with its ministers, be left to judge freely for itself as to the details of Christian doctrine and ritual? Would not this, too, exemplify, far more than is done at present, 'the unity of the spirit in the bond of peace'—the unity of a common reverence and love towards the Great Father of all, along with loyalty, trust, and aspiration towards his Christ, and this even in the midst of much, mutually permitted, diversity of thought and teaching and outward administration?

Alas, however, as it appears, it cannot be so yet. But this forms no real reproach to the Christian Master, to his spirit, or his religion. It is by our own human imperfection and manifold ignorance and perverseness that it is so. We are still left to feel that the spirit of Christ's life is high above us, and that we are not yet able, as the rule, with all our efforts and all our professions, to raise ourselves up to the attainment of that ideal.

Instead of this, we are naturally apt to follow and be contented with what is more within our reach. There is church authority, for example, the observance of rites and forms, the profession of creeds; and some persons would seem to go so far as even to push the Master aside from his spiritual headship, to substitute for him the words of other masters,— the growth, as these so notoriously are, of ill-informed and credulous ages. Those who are contented to do this, are not the persons for whom these pages are written; nor do I propose to address myself here to any elaborate discussion of such ideas. Doubtless time will show. The words of Christ remain to us, and will remain. The human creeds and confessions of later ages, which are not in harmony with his mind—the vast accumulations of 'wood and hay and stubble'—tried by the fire, shall be consumed and pass away and leave no trace behind. Men shall wonder in days to come that, amidst the angry discussions of our time, the thoughts of Christ and the lofty spirit of his life have been so strangely left out of sight; while Athanasian and other teaching which he never knew, on subjects which he and his apostles have only passed over with reverential silence, has been allowed to usurp the seat of authority which belongs to him—and all this, meantime, has been done in his name!

Christendom, however, let us nothing doubt, shall eventually find peace in a return to the simplicity of Christ. No other peace is now possible. Multitudes, ever increasing, of the most thoughtful men and women, have passed far beyond the authority of antiquated churches and priesthoods. They understand quite well that this is only another name for the authority of persons like themselves—of men, too, of past times, which, though largely hidden from our view by the obscuring shadows of a venerable antiquity, were yet, they also know, times of comparative ignorance and semi-barbarism. Moreover, is it not true that, even where the ancient ecclesiastical dogmas are professed, they are rarely *believed* in their full extent, or in the natural, that is, the original, sense of the words? Thus, for example, who, among Protestants believes in the 'communion of saints,' or the 'forgiveness of sins,' in the genuine sense of these propositions?* Who, among the tens of thousands that habitually repeat them in the Creed, ever even thinks of their

---

* The one meaning Participation in the superfluous merits of the saints, by their transfer to us; the other being a confession of the authority of the Church (the priest) to forgive sin.

true meaning, or cares much what it was? But when men have either come to neglect the proper import of a formal profession of faith, or feel themselves obliged to resort to forced and non-natural interpretations in order to retain it among them, can we reasonably doubt that its days are numbered, and that it cannot hold its ground among honourable men as a permanent expression of divine truth?

Christianity, then, let me further observe, is still destined to undergo a kind of development. It was so in the beginning and through many centuries,—a development which took place in those days according to the genius and the spirit, the knowledge or the ignorance, of the people amongst whom it was carried out. So it must still be; and the churches, having learnt wisdom, it may be hoped, from their wandering of many generations in the wilderness of manifold error and unfruitful dogmatism, have yet to return—or to go forward, shall I not rather say?—to the long-forgotten simplicity, grace, truth, and liberty of Christ's own teaching.

CHAPTER X.

FALLACIES AND OBJECTIONS.

It remains to take notice, somewhat more fully than has yet been done, of a common and twofold fallacy of our time. It is the error of identifying, too closely or exclusively, the simple, spiritual, and practical Gospel which Christ has placed before us, with the elaborate dogmatic Creeds and Confessions of modern theological systems. This is done by two very different classes of persons, and with very different purpose in each case.

On the one hand, it is perfectly natural for the defender of the ordinary orthodox theology, in its various forms, to seek to show that his creed is identical with the Christianity of Christ. Perhaps enough has been said in the foregoing pages to enable the reader to judge how far any one is entitled to hold this ground. If, on due inquiry, he shall find it to be so, he may reasonably say to himself, This theology, whether Roman Catholic, Calvinistic, Wesleyan or Anglican, and so on, shall be mine, because I find it to correspond truly with the words of the divine Teacher. But even so, a question remains; and it is, whether we ought not each to take our idea of Christ, his work and his religion, **direct from** him, as he stands before us in the Gospel?—whether in pure faith and loyalty to him we ought not to be well satisfied with that rich and varied store of instruction and influence, in precept, parable, discourse, exhortation and prayer, which he offers for our acceptance?—whether this in its native 'grace and truth,' as exemplified by Christ, is not really intended to be the Christian Gospel, and is not amply sufficient to make us 'wise unto salvation.'

It may, however, be asked, Shall we, then, leave all the rest of the New Testament out of sight to receive only what is contained in the Gospels? Would not this be imperfect and one-sided? To this question the answer has already been given by anticipation. Clearly we should use every means within our reach to gain a nearer access to Christ, whether it be an apostle, or an evangelist, or even a pagan or a Jewish historian, that offers to aid us. But there will be little wisdom in substituting for Christian teaching, ideas and doctrines manifestly derived from the subtleties of heathen philosophy or the metaphysics of the schoolmen. And I would also remind my reader of those words of Paul, 'Other foundation can no man lay than that is laid, which is Jesus Christ;' with those other words of his, 'Put ye on the Lord Jesus Christ;' and those other words again, in which he speaks of our advancing onward 'unto the measure of the stature of the fulness of Christ.' I would recall to him, further, the conception of the fourth Evangelist, who gives us that inquiry of the apostle Peter, 'Lord, to whom shall we go? Thou hast words of eternal life;' and that notable declaration of the Master himself, 'I am the way, the truth, and the life.' From such expressions it is clear that it will at least be apostolical to adhere very *closely* to Christ, and to regard him as the true representative and expression of his own religion. So doing, we shall without doubt be rid of many troublesome questions and controversies. The authority of 'the Church' may suffer, but Christianity will gain; various creeds and doctrines, about which a great noise is made in our day, may have to retire into comparative obscurity; but this will little matter, if in their place we get, with greater life and power, the Spirit and the Word of Christ himself.

But, on the other hand, it is tacitly assumed by a different class of persons, that the usual conception of Christianity, as especially and distinctively a very definite system of dogmatic teaching, is the *right* conception of it; and that the religion must be judged, to be accepted or rejected, precisely as that conception, in all its details and consequences, is found to be admissible at the bar of reason and moral sense. Those who thus sit in judgment on what they term the Gospel have usually a very obvious purpose.* They intend to do it as much damage as they can in the estimation of reflecting men.

* Strauss, it would appear, identifies Christianity with the Apostles' Creed, and finds, accordingly, that he has a very easy attack upon it. (Professor Scholten on Strauss, *Theological Review*, April, 1873.)

A recent very able writer, whose work (*Supernatural Religion, an Inquiry into the Reality of Divine Revelation*, 2 vols., 1874) I have not had the opportunity of perusing so fully as it deserves, expressly holds that Christianity 'distinctly pretends to be a direct Divine Revelation of truths beyond the natural attainment of the human intellect' (p. xiv.). This may be quite true of what the author terms 'ecclesiastical Christianity;' but where is such a claim put forth in the teaching of Jesus Christ? I must observe, too, that the word ' Revelation,' in the ' ecclesiastical ' sense in which it is commonly used, is conspicuous in the New Testament simply by its *absence*; and the same remark is true of the idea which that word usually conveys. Nor can I admit, in regard to the teaching of Christ, that the Gospel, as it came from *his* lips, is dependent upon the 'evidential force' of miracles, whatever this may be, or may be supposed to be. Does he ever work a miracle in order to prove the truth of a *doctrine*.

Strong, therefore, or even conclusive, as the argument of the work just cited may be, as against various authorities,— viz. Dr. Mozley, Archbishop Trench, Dr. J. H. Newman, and others,—yet I submit that the Christianity of Christ, as exhibited in the foregoing pages, is little touched by it. The intrinsic power of the Master's life and words is not due to the miracles related in connection with his personal history— related, be it observed, not by Christ himself, but by *others* who have written of him. On the contrary, the miraculous element attaches itself far less to the inner heart or ' essence ' of his teaching, than to the outer and non-essential circumstances amidst which this has been preserved and handed

Repelled and irritated, it may be, by the errors and corruptions which, under the Christian name, have still so much influence in the world,—anxious, at all costs, to put an end to these,—they are quite ready to admit that the Gospel is just that which its popular expounders would represent—neither more nor less. And being such, they hold it to be inadmissible as a theory of either God or man; inconsistent with the dictates of reason; in some points even an offence to moral feeling—as, for example, in its doctrine of an eternal hell.

How largely such considerations have sway among the more cultivated and thoughtful of the as yet

---

down to us. And this I may say, without intending to deny the reality of a miraculous element in the ministry of Christ. But, whatever this may have been, it was mainly or exclusively for those who *witnessed* it. For the men of our later times it has manifestly, in large degree, lost its power. Hence, those who cannot admit the miracles are simply in the position of men left to see and feel and interpret for themselves, with their own minds, the great spiritual truths and principles which formed, and form, the abiding substance of Christ's own Gospel. The ' witness of the spirit ' for God and His will is *within* rather than without—not in miraculous attestations which themselves require attestation, but in the rational assent of our own higher nature. Whatever of outward and material support may once have been felt to proceed from the former source, has been gradually falling away with advancing time and knowledge. But this, too, shall we not say, is God's own doing? He has willed, He is willing, that so it shall be! And is it not *our* highest wisdom to be ready to follow His providential guidance even in this?

unchristianized multitudes of India and other Eastern countries, it is unnecessary here to say; or how great an impediment such a conception of the Gospel is in the way of the evangelization of the world. But then the objection referred to, does it not proceed on a false assumption? With the life and teaching of Christ before us, is it possible to admit that Christianity is what these objectors would represent? Surely it is not; but the Gospel, as before, is to be judged, not by what over-zealous or ill-informed men have said of it, but by the actual life and teaching of its founder reasonably interpreted. It is not to be judged merely by the creeds or theologies so acceptable in our time,—the products as these are of minds which, however earnest and honest, were yet, it is well known, under the influence of the imperfect knowledge of their respective periods. The true idea of Christianity is not to be learnt from mediæval thinkers,* any more than from Arian and Athanasian controversialists. It is not to be learnt from the theories of an Augustin or an Anselm, any more than from the later conceptions of a Luther, a Calvin, or even a Wesley—worthy, learned, helpful, as doubtless many of these men were, and may still be. For they were not inspired. They had not received authority to speak in the

* The Athanasian Creed (as it is) cannot be traced back farther than the eighth century.

name of Christ, or to impose their private belief upon others. They were no more 'infallible' than the Pope himself. The true idea of Christianity is to be found, still and ever, within the pages of the New Testament; above and before all else, in the teaching and the spirit of Christ.

There is one further consideration: He in whom we have found so loftily exemplified the spiritual life which constitutes the most permanent and characteristic element of Christianity, is one who is richly entitled to be looked up to and spoken of with the sympathy, admiration, and reverence, due from the disciple to such a Master. Yet some, it would appear, even while they 'profess and call themselves Christians,' more or less hesitate in this very point —refusing to give to him the long-descended titles of Christ, and Lord, and Saviour, so gladly conferred upon him eighteen hundred years ago, by those who were most intimately acquainted with his character. There is an obvious inconsistency in this position. He who stands before us so conspicuously, the 'Chief of faithful souls,' and true King of men, in the highest sense of these words, may well receive the loyal recognition and homage of all who call themselves by his name; nor can it be unfitting to remember him and ask to partake of his spirit, even in the prayers which we address to 'his Father and our Father, his God and our God.'

That this due reverence towards the Christian Master must needs interfere with that highest honour and worship which belongs to God alone, is an embarrassment which, it may be thought, but few minds of any true spiritual capacity can really feel. For how can sympathy with Christ, in his spirit of love for God and man, or how can the remembrance of his devout and self-sacrificing life, be an impediment, or anything but a help, to the more intimate communion between the human soul and its Father in heaven? To most of us, in fact, Christ has largely been Teacher, Guide and Saviour,* even though, in some cases, we may have scarcely known it or acknowledged it ourselves,—as to multitudes, again, the thought of him has often given strength

> * 'Great Chief of faithful souls! arise:
> None else can lead the martyr-band,
> Who teach the brave, how peril flies,
> When Faith, unarmed, uplifts the hand.
>
> O King of earth! the cross ascend:
> O'er climes and ages 'tis thy throne:
> Where'er thy fading eye may bend,
> The desert blooms, and is thine own.
>
> Thy parting blessing, Lord, we pray;
> Make but one fold below, above:
> And when we go the last lone way,
> O give the welcome of thy love.'
>
> *Hymns of Praise and Prayer*, edited by Dr. James Martineau, 1874: No. 133.

and peace divine amidst the hardest trials of human life.

Truly, then, may we each look up to him and speak of him as Christ our Lord, the anointed King in spiritual things. We need not, indeed, put him in the place of GOD, or attach idolatrous meanings to the terms and phrases we employ respecting him. So to do is quite unnecessary, as it would in fact be directly contrary to his own express precepts and example. But that many run into such unwarrantable extremes of error, will not justify us in coldly doing the reverse; and assuredly it need not repel us from any words of affectionate reverence and gratitude by which we may best exalt his name, and render a just tribute to his memory.

But, let it be freely admitted nevertheless, if any modern authority, of whatever school, can show us 'a more excellent way' than that which Christ has pointed out, it will be our duty to walk in this better light; to govern and control our lives by those higher principles of righteousness, truth, and love, which it may have been reserved for any earnest religious soul of our times to set before the world. But until these have been given, it may not be amiss to adhere still to the highest and best which we have got; and is not this much the same thing as saying that we should still strive, though it may be with feeble and faltering step, to follow Him in whom the Almighty Father was well pleased, and who himself the best has shown us the way to the Eternal Peace?

APPENDIX.

A.—Non-Christian Testimonies respecting Jesus Christ.

The following are the earliest statements which occur respecting the Founder of Christianity.

(1.) Tacitus probably wrote his *Annals* about the close of the first century of our era. This work relates to the period from the death of Augustus to the close of the reign of Nero, 68, A.D. In Book xv. c. 44, the historian speaks of the persecution of the Christians under the latter emperor, and gives a very graphic account of their sufferings. He says, they were commonly called 'Christians,' and adds,—'The originator of this name was Christus, who, in the reign of Tiberius, was punished with death by the procurator Pontius Pilate.'

(2.) Suetonius was a younger contemporary of Tacitus, and wrote his Lives of the Roman Emperors early in the second century. In his life of Claudius, he very probably refers to Jesus Christ in the following words: The Emperor, he says, 'expelled the Jews from Rome, as they were continually causing disturbances, Chrestus being their instigator.' If Jesus Christ be here meant, the statement is evidently very inaccurate, for he had been dead many years before the time of Claudius, who died in 54, A.D., after a reign of thirteen years. The words may, however, be understood of controversies and disturbances between the Jews and the Christians in Rome; and a heathen historian might suppose that those who, from their founder, were called 'Christiani' were still under his leadership, or at least under the influence of his teaching. The Romans would readily attribute a political character both to the religious belief of the Christians, and to any troubles arising from their controversies with the Jews. They were not unaware of the Messianic expectations of the latter, as shown by a statement of Tacitus (Hist. v. 13), to the effect that they believed it to have been foretold in the sacred books of their priests that the East should at that time become mighty, and that princes to arise from Judea should possess the empire of the world. Which obscure oracle, however, the historian not unreasonably adds, was to be interpreted of his own emperors Vespasian and Titus.

These allusions, it is evident, add nothing of importance to the evangelical narratives, while yet they serve to confirm their statements in several particulars. One point only may here be noticed. It is, that Jesus was known to the Romans, not by the name of Jesus, but simply as *Christus*. Of the former name there is no trace whatever in these writers. The remark is of use in connection with the passage from Josephus mentioned below.

(3.) In the Letters of PLINY the younger (A.D. 109) there is a passage which speaks of the Christians of his province of Bithynia. After noticing the obstinacy of many in adhering to their Christian confession, he mentions others who had been induced to worship the emperor's image and the statues of the gods, and to revile Christ. Some of these apostates informed Pliny that the Christians 'were accustomed to meet together on a stated day, before it was light, and to sing a hymn to Christ as if to a god' (carmenque Christo, quasi deo, dicere). This statement and the connection in which it is found indicates the high honour in which Christ was held at the beginning of the second century. It does not, however, show that the Bithynian Christians worshipped him as GOD. The word *deus* in the mouth of a Roman proconsul would have no such lofty meaning, for it is well known that it was used, both by Greek and Latin writers, in a far lower sense than is the corresponding word by ourselves at the present day. Yet it is quite probable that, even in the time of Pliny, many Gentile converts to Christianity were beginning to speak of Jesus Christ and to honour him as a sort of inferior God. So to do would be in perfect harmony with their previous ideas of the 'gods many and lords many' (1 Cor. viii. 5) of their heathen idolatry.

(4.) JOSEPHUS, the Jewish historian, wrote in Greek, about the year 90, A.D., his account of the Jewish nation. Writing, as he did, expressly for Roman readers, to whom at least the terms *Christ* and *Christian* were, as we have seen, well known, it would have been very strange if he had omitted altogether to mention the new sect, or even to give some brief account of its origin. This omission, however, he does not make. For he not only mentions John the Baptist as a righteous man who had been put to death by Herod, but, when speaking of the time of Pontius Pilate, he gives us the following statement:

"About this time lived Jesus, a wise man, if it be proper to call him a man. For he was a doer of surprising deeds, a teacher of men who willingly receive what is true. And many Jews and many also of the Greek race he brought to his side. This was the Christ; and those who had at first loved him did not cease to do so, when Pilate, on the accusation of the chief men among us, punished him with the cross. For he appeared to them on the third day alive again, the divine prophets having spoken both this and very many other wonderful things concerning him. To this day the party of the Christians who have been named from him have not ceased to exist." (*Antiq*. xviii. 3, 3.)

This passage is found in all the extant manuscripts of Josephus, and it is known to have been so from the time of Eusebius, A.D. 300–340. Yet its authenticity has been doubted by Lardner and others, upon grounds which I cannot here attempt to state in detail, but which, I must add, appear to me to be far from conclusive. It is not necessary in estimating its value, to suppose that Josephus is expressing his *own* belief, as to either the character or the works of Jesus; or to think that he intended to acknowledge him as the Christ, although at first sight he appears to say this. Most probably he is only giving what was currently said, and generally known to be said, by the Christians: and the words, 'this was the Christ,' are simply equivalent to the statement, 'this was the person so well known to the Romans under the name of Christus.' It would be impossible for Josephus to believe that a crucified man had really been the expected Messiah. When he terms Jesus 'a wise man, if it be proper to call him a man,' this does not necessarily imply the idea that he may really have been a god, as the Christians might, some of them, be affirming. It may be reasonably supposed to allude to the possibility of his having been one of the ancient prophets come back from the dead, an idea that was familiar to the Jews of Christ's time (Luke ix. 7-9). In this light Josephus might readily have regarded him, though not in the exalted character of Messiah.

The subject is one of some extent and difficulty, and I must, therefore, be contented with this expression of my own opinion that the passage is in the main authentic, though it may not be possible to prove that it is wholly genuine, as it now stands. I may notice, however, that a Christian interpolator would most probably have written, not 'what is true,' but rather 'the truth;' similarly he would have spoken not of those who 'loved him,' but of 'those who believed on him;' and surely such an interpolator would have used a stronger expression than, 'have not ceased to exist.'

B.—PASSAGES IN THE PAULINE EPISTLES WHICH APPEAR TO SPEAK OF JESUS CHRIST AS GOD.

Such passages are only two in number; and in reality they bear and require a different interpretation—as will probably be seen from the following statement of the facts.

(1.) Rom. ix. 5: 'Whose are the fathers, and of whom, as concerning the flesh, Christ came, who is God over all, blessed for ever,'—so the English authorized version. In the Greek, the order of the words is a little different, thus: 'Whose are the fathers, and of whom the Christ came, as concerning the flesh, who [or he who] is God over all blessed for ever.' The words are and came do not occur in the original. The verse may be correctly translated thus: 'Whose are the fathers, and of whom is the Christ, as concerning the flesh. He who is God over all is blessed for ever. Amen.'

The reader is probably aware that the most ancient manuscripts of the New Testament are, for the most part, without stops, and even have the words running together without break. Thus the Vatican MS., mentioned below, reads part of the verse under notice thus:

ΤΟΚΑΤΑΣΑΡΚΑΟΩΝΕΠΙΠΑΝΤΩΝΘΣ.

Hence the possibility of a doubt, in some cases, as to where a division should be made, or what kind of stop should be inserted. In the present case I may add that, having the opportunity, some little time ago, of examining the celebrated Vatican manuscript (B), one of the two most ancient codices of the New Testament, I found in it a *stop* after the word ΣΑΡΚΑ (flesh); the same stop which is found in many other instances in the same manuscript, dividing the words of a sentence; the same, in fact, which is used after the word *Amen* at the end of the verse. In accordance with this stopping, which is unquestionably of great antiquity, although it may not have proceeded from the actual writer of the manuscript, the words may be translated as I have given them above, substantially following the rendering of Prof. Jowett—(*Epistles of St. Paul*, in loco).

It is not difficult to see the idea under which the Apostle is writing. He enumerates the great privileges of his people, including the birth from among them of the expected Messiah, who, he says, by natural descent was a Jew. This leads him to break forth into what is in effect an ascription of praise to Him who is the Giver of every blessing. The clause in which he does so is similar in form to words in 2 Cor. xi. 31, which run thus: 'The God and Father of our Lord Jesus Christ knoweth, he who is blessed for ever, that I lie not.' Here there can be no uncertainty as to who is meant by the words, 'he who is blessed for ever.' It can only be 'the God and Father of our Lord Jesus Christ.' Nor should there be really any doubt to an unbiassed mind respecting the other verse. The apostle Paul *never*, in any other instance, terms Jesus Christ *God;* and the analogy of his writings and style ought alone to forbid the supposition that he does so here. This is admitted by the great (orthodox) German commentator, Meyer; it is recognized by Tischendorf, who, I suppose, is equally 'orthodox,' and who places a full stop after the word 'flesh;' it is recognized by Lachmann, by De Wette, by Professor Holzmann, the editor of Bunsen's *Bibelwerk*, and by Ewald, all these being among the most eminent of modern authorities on the subject. The admissibility of the rendering given above is admitted by Winer (*New Testament Grammar*, by Moulton, p. 690). The argument of some, *e.g.* Dean Alford, Dr. Liddon, Dr. C. J. Vaughan, for the common rendering, from the later position in the sentence of the word 'blessed,' is scarcely worthy of serious examination in the face of the opposing considerations, and may even be said to be one which could only be put forward under the pressure of great theological necessity. The word thus rendered, moreover, εὐλογητός, is applied in the New Testament to the Almighty only, never to Jesus Christ. The presumption, therefore, is very strong that it is not so applied here. The peculiar form of the sentence, as regards the position of the word 'blessed,' is amply allowed for and expressed by the rendering of Professor Jowett as above given; while the parallel phrase in 2 Cor. xi. 31, although the words are not, properly speaking, a doxology, surely far outweighs even the '30 passages of the Septuagint' in which, it has been observed, a different order of words occurs. And must it not be considered a somewhat weak feature in what may be termed the popular acceptation of the passage, that it should have to take refuge and find its main support, not, so to speak, in the real merits of the case, but in an inference from the mere order of the words?

Finally, it may be permitted to me to quote the following words from the work mentioned in the Preface to this volume:—'The German commentator Meyer, perhaps the highest living authority on a point of this kind, while himself a believer in the deity of Christ, maintains that the doxology cannot be referred to Christ, but to God only. St. Paul, he reminds us, has never applied the term θεός to Christ, although, as Meyer holds, he *might*, in accordance with his own belief, have done so. On the contrary, the line of distinction between the Father and the Son is so observed throughout the New Testament, that the appellation God is everywhere applied only to the Father, except in two instances (duly considered in these pages), namely, John i. 1 and xx. 28, [see *supra*, Chap. VII.,] both of which occur in immediate connection with the Logos idea. This learned commentator further notices that it was not until after the apostolical times that the distinction just alluded to disappeared, and that the words, ὁ θεός, ὁ θεὸς ἡμῶν (God, our God), and similar expressions, were used of Christ.' (*Bible and Popular Theology*, 3rd ed., p. 199.)

(2.) Philip. ii. 6: 'Who being in the form of God, thought it not robbery to be equal with God, but made himself of no reputation,' &c. This rendering is not perfectly accurate. The words should run thus: 'Who being in the form of God [or, a god] did not think the being equal to God [or, a god] a thing to be eagerly seized, but made himself of no reputation,' &c.* Here Christ is not expressly termed God, but many think that he is represented as having given up the 'prerogatives' of his Deity, and humbled himself. This very gross anthropomorphic conception of the Infinite, which represents Him who 'is a Spirit,' 'the high and lofty One that inhabit-

---

* Compare Dean Alford's rendering—'Who being in the form of God, deemed not his equality with God a thing to grasp at.' The word *his* is here inserted without authority and without necessity. (*N. T. Revised*.)

eth eternity,' as laying aside the glories of his divine nature, to live in obscurity as a man upon the earth, may pass here for what it is worth. It cannot be necessary with thoughtful readers to comment upon it. The passage, nevertheless, is obscure and difficult. But the following may be something like the idea which the Apostle intended to convey. Jesus was born and lived in humble circumstances. He was delivered up into the hands of his enemies, and crucified as a malefactor. But yet he was the Messiah; and as such entitled of right to all the glories which the popular belief had associated with that exalted office. He might have been even as a god upon earth, in his majesty and power. But all this he had renounced; 'though he was rich,' yet 'he became poor' (2 Cor. viii. 9); living a life of poverty and shame. Although, as the Messiah, 'in the form of God' (or, perhaps, 'in the form of a god'), *i.e.* either the representative on earth of God, or else, by virtue of his Messianic character like a god among men, entitled to so high a place,—yet, for the sake of others, he stooped to the lowest humiliation, the death upon the cross; he had done this in obedience to the Divine will, and out of his own lowliness, self-renunciation, and love for sinful men. For this, said the Apostle, 'God hath highly exalted him, and given him a name which is above every name;' that *in* his name (not '*at*,' which is a mistranslation) 'every knee should bow,' and every tongue confess him to be Lord, 'to the glory of God the Father.'

All this is in perfect harmony with the distinction everywhere expressed or implied by St. Paul between God and Christ; the one being the supreme God and Father of all, 'the God and Father of Jesus Christ;' the other, the lowly messenger and servant of the Divine Will, the Son of the Divine Love, whose very words were not his own, and whose meat it was to do the will of Him that sent him, and to finish his work.

(3.) 1 Tim. iii. 16: '. . . Great is the mystery of godliness; God was manifest in the flesh,' &c. The word 'God' is here rejected by the best modern authorities. Dean Alford renders, '... Great is the mystery of godliness, who was manifested in the flesh,' &c. He adds the remark: 'So all the most ancient authorities, except one which reads *which*, neuter gender.' (*New Testament, Revised Translation*.) Bishop Ellicott (*Pastoral Epistles*, in loco) closes his review of the passage with the observation, 'We unhesitatingly decide in favour of 'ὅς' (*who*, or *he who*).

C.

(1.) *Acts* xx. 28: '.... to feed the church of God, which he hath purchased with his own blood.' The ancient manuscript evidence is here divided as to whether the reading should be 'God' or 'the Lord.' Recent writers of the highest authority (*e.g.* Tischendorf) prefer the latter. Among commentators, Meyer may be especially named as taking the same side, while Dean Alford with many others decide for the more orthodox reading. The two reputedly most ancient Greek MSS. have 'God.' These are the *Codex Vaticanus* already mentioned, and the *Codex Sinaiticus*. The latter is judged by Tischendorf to be the oldest MS. of the Greek text in existence, while the Vatican is not much later. Granting that this is so, and it follows that these MSS. were written in the same century (perhaps even, one of them, in the same half of the century) which witnessed the Nicene Council,—a period, it is well known, of eager controversy as to the person of Christ, and in which it was decreed by the majority of an assembly of theologians (of whose judicial fitness for their office the reader may judge who will consult Dean Stanley's *History of the Eastern Church*), that Jesus Christ is *God* in a certain secondary sense, 'God of God,' as stated in the Nicene Creed. Remembering these facts, it is impossible to avoid the question whether some orthodox copyist of that age of theological strife and persecution may not have taken it upon himself to conform his copy to the predominant belief of his time? Can any one, in the face

L

of the evidence for 'Lord,' say with confidence that it may not have been so? Nor is this case the only one in the New Testament in which an alteration in the reputedly orthodox direction has almost certainly been made. For example, there is the reading of one of these very MSS. (the C. Sinaiticus), in Luke viii. 40, where, instead of saying, 'they were all waiting for him' (*i.e.* for Jesus), the verse runs, 'they were all waiting for *God*.' Can such a change have been unintentional? The reader will also remember 1 Tim. iii. 16 and 1 John v. 7, both of which have an equally suspicious character.

The 'blood of the Lord,' by which, in a certain sense, the church was purchased, is an expression, the literal meaning of which is determinable from the historical considerations set forth above, in Chapter VI. The 'blood of God' is not admissible with any due regard to religious reverence; though doubtless it might be acceptable to a Gentile Christian whose mind was full of the Logos doctrine,—a doctrine which, in that same century, had attained the height of its influence.

(2.) In connection with the last passage may be mentioned another remarkable reading, possibly also introduced under the same Nicene influences. It is in John i. 18, where both the manuscripts before named read 'only begotten god' for 'only begotten Son.' The latter is the undoubted reading of various important MSS., versions, and Fathers—insomuch that it is a question of some nicety to determine on which side the greater weight of critical evidence lies. The reader will find an able discussion of the point in the *Theological Review*, 1871, page 469, *seq.*

So far as the general character of this Gospel is concerned, either reading is quite admissible. Doubtless, the Logos is meant in either case; and, as we have seen (Chap. VII.), this was sometimes spoken of as 'God,' or 'a god.' Should the reading under notice be considered to be established, the resulting form of the English text will be at least an unhappy one. The text must also be corrected by the omission (on the same authority) of the definite article. The rendering of the verse will thus be, 'No man hath seen God, at any time; an only begotten god, which is in the bosom of the Father, he hath declared him.' This, it can scarcely be doubted, will tend, in the judgment of many thoughtful readers, to cast a shadow upon the common doctrine of the deity of Jesus Christ.

(3.) 1 John v. 20: 'This is the true God and eternal life.' The word 'this' may very probably be referred to the remoter antecedent, *i.e.* to 'him that is true.' Compare 2 John v. 7, where a similar construction occurs: 'This is a [the] deceiver and an [the] anti-Christ,' said apparently of the Lord Jesus Christ.

D.

(1.) Titus ii. 13: 'Looking for that blessed hope and the glorious appearing of the great God and our Saviour Jesus Christ.' Dean Alford (*New Testament Revised*) renders, 'the manifestation of the glory of the great God and of our Saviour Jesus Christ.' Mr. Sharpe (*New Testament* from Griesbach's Text, 6th ed.) has, 'appearing of the glory of the great God and of our Saviour Jesus Christ.' These translations, like many others (as those of Bunsen and De Wette) distinguish between 'God' and 'Jesus Christ,' intending respectively to denote two different objects, or persons, and not one only. On the other hand, some authorities (as Bishop Ellicott, *Pastoral Epistles*, in loco) render thus: 'Looking for the blessed hope and appearing of the glory of our great God and Saviour Jesus Christ.' The Greek, it is usually acknowledged, may be correctly represented by *either* translation. The unlearned reader may well be contented to follow the analogy of the usual tenor of St. Paul's Epistles, which, as before observed, distinguish carefully between God and Christ. This it is the more easy to do, seeing that the judgment of such scholars as Meyer and Winer is on the side of the rendering followed in our common version.

(2.) 2 Peter i. 1: 'Through the righteousness of God and

our Saviour Jesus Christ.' A corrected Greek Text may be rendered thus: 'Through the righteousness of our God and Saviour Jesus Christ'—though this is in one respect a decided over-rendering. But the remarks just made in reference to Tit. ii. 13, are applicable in the present case. Winer and Meyer both pronounce against the latter rendering, and it is rejected by De Wette, Bunsen, and Ewald. These authorities hold that the insertion of the definite article 'the' before 'Saviour' is required,—just as it is before the words 'Holy Spirit,' in Matt. i. 18, and some similar cases. Dean Alford renders 'the righteousness of our God and [our] Saviour Jesus Christ,' in this following some of the ancient versions, including the Syriac.

From the foregoing summary of the evidence on the subject, under the heads B, C, D, it is evident that neither the apostle Paul, nor any other New Testament writer, speaks of Jesus Christ under the designation of God. So far as this may appear to occur in the fourth Gospel, it is to be remembered that it is really the Logos which is so designated. In what sense, and under what influences, this was done, has been sufficiently pointed out in the chapter relating to the subject.

E.—ON THE TITLES 'SON OF MAN' AND 'SON OF GOD.'

(1.) The former of these occurs many times in the Old Testament, as *e.g.* in Ezekiel, where it is usually the form in which Jehovah addresses the prophet. It is simply equivalent to *man* or *human being*. In the New Testament it has a more specific meaning. In every instance in which it occurs in the Gospels, it is employed by Jesus Christ to designate himself. Besides the Gospels, it is only found in Acts vii. 56, and in Rev. i. 13, xiv. 14; being used, in all these cases, by the writer of the book in speaking of Jesus in his risen state.

The origin of the phrase is, no doubt, to be found in Dan. vii. 13, where the writer says that he saw visions, 'and behold one like [a] Son of Man came with the clouds of heaven, and came to the ancient of days.' This verse was understood of the Messiah and his kingdom. The association of the 'clouds of heaven' with the Son of Man is found also in Rev. xiv. 14; and the same is probably the conception of Matt. xxv. 31. The Book of Enoch uses the same expression to denote the Messiah, and speaks of his coming in the same terms which occur in the passage of Matt. xxv. 31, *seq*. The Book of Enoch, although in parts, it is believed, interpolated, is most probably in those which speak of the Son of Man of older date than our Gospels. This, again, may be regarded as showing that the phrase was in use among the Jews before the ministry of Christ began, and that the words were simply an appellation of the Messiah derived, as before stated, from Dan. vii. 13.

According to these facts, the phrase has no recondite or mystical meaning whatever. It was not intended either to denote the lowly condition of the Messiah, or to convey the suggestion that he was a typical man, the most perfect example of the human race. However true any one may deem the latter idea, still it is not to be based upon the use of this expression; and, so far as this is concerned, it is a mere fancy of interpreters, wholly destitute of corroborative evidence.

Jesus, then, by the phrase under notice, designated himself as the *Messiah*, according to the usual understanding of those to whom he spoke. It has been a question, whether, in some of the earlier instances of its use, he may not have intended to designate, not himself, but a third person,—*i.e.*, the expected Messiah, whom accordingly he distinguishes from himself. For this supposition there is no sufficient evidence; and, on the whole, we may understand that, in every case, the speaker by this title meant himself, and in using it assumed the character of Messiah, in whatever sense he may have done so. It is, however, a distinct and important question, how far he really did so frequently use the expression, or how far we owe the constant introduction of the words to the choice of the Evangelist—to the literary form, that is to say, into which he has chosen to put his narrative. Upon this question I do not propose further to enter.

(2.) The origin of the second title is more obscure. Yet in the Old Testament it is by no means uncommon. The collective Israel is termed the 'Son' of God. So Exod. iv. 22, 23; Hos. xi. 1, and similarly Jerem. xxxi. 20. Kings, as vicegerents of God on earth, are designated as 'Sons;' so in Ps. lxxxii. 6, comp. Ps. lxxxix. 27. Solomon is emphatically so termed, 2 Sam. vii. 14. The same appellation was applicable in an eminent degree to the Messiah. It is accordingly used of him in an ancient Messianic passage, viz. Ps. ii. 7 (comp. v. 2). Hence again the expression is used in the Book of Enoch in reference to the same personage, who in one instance (cap. 105) is designated by the Almighty as 'my Son.'

What is thus more especially implied or denoted by the term, as thus employed, is the fatherly protection, favour and love of God for his chosen vicegerent, the Prince Messiah. There is no reason whatever to understand it as expressive of any more intimate or metaphysical relationship.

In many of the New Testament books there can be no question that these words are used in this simply Messianic and historical sense. The Messiah was naturally conceived of as pre-eminently the Son of God; and Jesus, as being the Messiah, was therefore the Son, and the 'beloved Son.' These terms are clearly, in many cases, convertible terms. Thus it is, sometimes, even in the writings of John; as John i. 49, Nathaniel, having been an unbeliever in the Messiahship, becomes a believer, and at once exclaims, 'Rabbi, thou art the Son of God; thou art the King of Israel.' It is impossible to think that the speaker here attributes any deep metaphysico-theological meaning to the words which he uses. So, John xi. 27, Martha says, ' I believe that thou art the Christ, the Son of God.' In 1 John, v. 1, 5, the expressions are similarly interchanged: 'Whosoever believeth that Jesus is the Christ, is born of God:' 'Who is he that overcometh the world, but he that believeth that Jesus is the Son of God?'

In other passages of the New Testament this Messianic signification is equally clear. Satan (Matt. iv. 3), says, 'If thou be [the] Son of God,' evidently meaning nothing more than, If thou be Messiah, as may be seen from the whole context. In Matt. xvi. 16, Peter exclaims, 'Thou art the Christ, the Son of the living God;' immediately afterwards, in v. 20, the disciples are charged 'that they should tell no man that he was Jesus the Christ.' At the trial, the high-priest says, 'Tell us whether thou be the Christ, the Son of God.' Pilate asked precisely the same question, in different terms, when he said, 'Art thou the king of the Jews?' (Matt. xxvi. 63; compare John xviii. 33, 37). The latter Evangelist writes (xx. 31), 'that ye may believe that Jesus is the Christ, the Son of God.' Acts ix. 20, Paul is stated to have 'preached Jesus* in the synagogues that he is the Son of God;' while, in a subsequent verse (22), the same apostle "confounded the Jews that dwelt at Damascus, proving that this [man] is Christ.' What Paul is said to have preached in the one case, and proved in the other, was the same thing, viz., that Jesus was the 'Son of God'—in other words, that he was the 'Christ.' In accordance with this exposition ought to be interpreted the words of Mark i. 1, 'the Gospel of Jesus Christ, [the] Son of God'—otherwise, 'the Gospel of Jesus Christ, the Messiah,'—in case, that is to say, the words 'Son of God' are retained. Their authenticity is very doubtful, and possibly they indicate the same growth of doctrine which is alluded to in the note.

* *Jesus* is the reading here, not *Christ*, according to the critical authorities. The substitution of *Christ* illustrates the development of doctrine, and shows us how, in time, Jesus was said to be not only Christ, or Son of God, but also Christ *and* Son of God, as though the two latter appellations were not in truth the *same*. A similar, perhaps unintended, divergence from primitive fact may be observed in Bishop Wordsworth's articles, 'Son of Man,' and 'Son of God,' in Dr. W. Smith's Dictionary of the Bible; and in the article 'Jesus Christ' in the same work, by Archbishop Thomson, p. 1,068. The same is also seen in Acts viii. 37, but this verse is an acknowledged interpolation.

In the synoptics, our Lord does not himself use the phrase 'Son of God.' It is applied to him, in a few cases, by others, and clearly in the Messianic sense. So the demoniacs, Matt. viii. 29; the people in the ship, xiv. 33, exclaim, 'Of a truth thou art [the] Son of God.' The centurion at the cross uses the same expression (Matt. xxvii. 54), although he was a person who could only have applied it in the Messianic sense, if even in that.

The title in question, as applied to the Messiah, may, as before observed, have originated in Ps. ii. 2, 7—one of the most ancient of the Psalms: comp. Acts xiii. 33, Heb. i. 5. Being thus of Hebrew origin, it coincided, however (accidentally), with one of the appellations of the Logos, although in a very different sense. In the latter case, the metaphysical or philosophical sense of the word 'Son' is unquestionable. Enough has been said upon this in the chapter relating to the subject; and it need only be observed here that from both points of view, the Hebrew and the Greek (or philosophical), Jesus would be the Son of God. The fourth Evangelist, accordingly, speaks of him, or at least of the Logos in him, as the 'only begotten Son;' perhaps even (i. 18), as 'an only begotten god'—a use of the phrase which immediately followed from the Logos doctrine adopted by this Evangelist. It is only the fourth or Logos Gospel which has the phrase 'only begotten' used of Christ. Compare 1 John iv. 9.

In one passage in the synoptics, there is an approach to this. It is in Luke i. 35, where Jesus is expressly termed 'Son of God' because of his conception by the Holy Spirit. Such is the idea of the writer of the passage. It was an obvious idea, and the wonder is that it never recurs in the New Testament, at least in the two Gospels of Matthew and Luke. It could not have failed to do so, had the miraculous conception been accepted in the earliest Christian times as an important and well-established fact of the evangelical history. Compare *supra*, Chap. I.

From the foregoing exposition it clearly results that the two phrases, 'Son of Man' and 'Son of God,' were, in their original and proper use, simply appellations of the

Messiah, and equivalent, in reality, to the term *Christ*, or *Anointed* (comp. Ps. ii. 2, 7). This is also the probable meaning of the latter of the two phrases as it occurs in the Pauline Epistles. In the writings of John we have a different conception (as also in the one verse of Luke, i. 35). The Logos in Jesus is, in John, the Son of God, in the highest metaphysical sense; and therefore Jesus is spoken of, and represented by this Evangelist as speaking of himself, under the same designation. But yet he is nowhere, even in this Gospel, represented as *Supreme God*. This greatest of appellations is everywhere strictly confided to the 'One God the Father'—τὸν μονον ἀληθινὸν Θεόν 'the Only True God.'*

F. ON THE MEANING OF JOHN VIII. 58.

'BEFORE Abraham was, I am;' or, more fully, 'Before Abraham came into existence, I am.' The words have been understood as an assertion by the speaker of his own self-existence, made with an implied allusion to Exod. iii. 14. This reference, however, is quite fallacious. The Hebrew verb in Exodus may be rendered as a *future*, 'I will be; and it is so given by the ancient Greek translators Aquila and Theodotion, both of whom are remarkable for the literal character of their renderings. The words are similarly translated by other authorities, ancient and modern. The English version of Exod. iii. 14 has followed the Vulgate, which no doubt imitated the Septuagint. The latter, however, is not ἐγώ εἰμι, I am, but ἐγώ εἰμι ὁ ὤν, 'I am he who is.' The words ὁ ὤν are the essential words for expressing the idea of self-existence; but they do not occur in John viii 58; nor is there anything to show that Jesus referred to the Greek Septuagint, in his conversations with the Pharisees in Jerusalem, by whom, most probably, that version was not used, even if they were acquainted with it. At all events,

* 1 Cor. viii. 6; John xvii. 3.

the more important words, ὁ ὤν, are left out; and in truth there is no more reason to suppose that, in saying ἐγώ εἰμι, he had Exod. iii. 14 in his mind than there is for saying the same thing of the blind man who also employs this expression in John ix. 9.

The specific meaning of these words must, therefore, be sought in the Gospel itself, and in the context of the passage more particularly. The key text for their interpretation may be found in the conversation with the woman of Samaria (iv. 25–26). She says, 'I know that Messias cometh, which is called Christ;' and Jesus replies, 'I that speak unto thee AM.' In John viii. 24 he says to the Jews, 'If ye believe not that I AM, ye shall die in your sins;' and again in viii. 28, 'When ye have lifted up the son of man, then ye shall know that I AM.' So in xiii. 19, 'Now I tell you before it come, that when it is come to pass ye may believe that I AM' (comp. 13). In these expressions the speaker asserts his Messiahship, and our English Translators have recognized this by inserting the word *he* in each case. The same form of expression occurs in Mark xiii. 6, 'Many shall come in my name saying, I AM.' i.e., 'I am *he*.' In these cases there can be no doubt as to the import of the words 'I am,' or that they are used to denote the Messiahship. But yet, as before observed, they take their specific meaning from their immediate context, and do not necessarily, in themselves, convey that idea; as where the blind man, merely asserting his own identity, uses the same words and says, 'I am *he*' (ix. 9). In all the cases just referred to, however, the context seems to justify, or require the Messianic meaning. And the same, I apprehend, is true of viii. 58. In this context, too, from v. 22 onward, Jesus is evidently asserting his claim to be received and believed, *i.e.*, in his character of Messiah. Or, if any one shall prefer to say, in his character of the Logos, it comes to the same thing, for he was the Messiah, in this Evangelist's conception, by the indwelling of the Logos. In the latter part of this chapter the Jews ask, '*Whom* makest thou thyself?' (v. 53), and he also declares, 'Abraham rejoiced to see *my* day," *i.e.*, the day of the Messiah (v. 56). The idea of his Messianic office is, therefore, clearly present to him, and affords an easy clue to the meaning of the words of v. 58. These, accordingly, may be understood to mean, 'Before Abraham came into existence, I am *he*;' I am the Messiah, though you, the unbelieving Jews, do not admit my claim: I am the Messiah fore-ordained to be so, in the divine counsels before Abraham existed. For a similar reference to pre-existence compare John xvii. 5.

It has been objected that there would be no propriety in the enforcement of the Messianic claim, when Jesus was addressing those who 'believed in him' (ver. 31). But this loses its weight as the dialogue proceeds. The Evangelist's notion of the audience changes, for he makes Jesus say, 'Why do ye not believe me' (ver. 46); and then, shortly after, they tell him that they know he has a devil (ver. 52). It cannot be said that under these circumstances a declaration of Messianic dignity was out of place. Indeed, it is much more what might have been expected than a mere assertion of pre-existence; and it seems the natural answer to the question in ver. 53.

Nevertheless, it may be freely admitted, the expression would receive an ample interpretation from a due regard to the Logos doctrine alone. See *supra*, chap. vii. The divine Word which 'became flesh' in Jesus (i. 14) existed 'in the beginning' with God: this was 'before Abraham,' and it may be simply this again, here, as in some other places, that the Evangelist has in his mind. But, on the whole, the preferable conclusion seems to be that the words 'I am' should here be taken in the same sense which they so obviously bear in the other places above cited, where Jesus is himself the speaker. See, however, an article on this subject by the Rev. J. Kenrick in the *Theological Review*, April, 1875, p. 306.

FINIS.

www.ingramcontent.com/pod-product-compliance
Lightning Source LLC
Chambersburg PA
CBHW030300170426
43202CB00009B/819